What to Cook for Dinner (with Kids)

How to Simplify, Strategize and Stop Agonizing over Family Dinners

Maryann Jacobsen, MS, RD

DEDICATION

For my mom, whose unconditional love made me who I am.

And for all the parents who struggle to get meals on the table and feel good about this thing called family dinner. May the struggle *finally* end.

CONTENTS

ACKNOWLEDGMENTS

A special thanks to all the parents who took the time to review the manuscript and try recipes. You made this book ten times better. And to my blog readers who inspire all that I do, thanks for your dedication to Raise Healthy Eaters and the health and well-being of your family. Thanks to Meg Salvia and my husband Dan Jacobsen, for attention to detail in editing. A big shout-out to the food blogs and websites that allowed me to share their recipes (too many to list). Thank you, thank you, thank you! I am also appreciative of the Cookbook People who generously donated their wonderful products. This book would never have come to light without my kids, Little D and Big A. You both make me a better cook *and* a better person.

A Million Recipes with Nothing to Cook

Imagine knowing exactly what to cook for dinner every night. Not only that, you feel good about these meals because you have made them before and know they are tasty, nutritious and provide just the right variety. There are no cooking surprises ("what, I needed to chill this??") or running out of ingredients. You know exactly how to serve these meals to kids to increase the likelihood they will accept them. And even if they don't, you have side dishes to go along with each meal that get the job done. You can sit back and enjoy this time with your family because you know exactly *what to cook for dinner* in a way that fits your life.

Unfortunately, this is not how dinner goes for most families. Instead, every night, many parents agonize over what to cook for dinner. This what-to-cook dilemma remains constant even with the Internet full of recipes and an explosion of family cookbooks lining bookshelves (and Amazon).

About seven years ago, I joined the ranks of families struggling to get meals on the table. My daughter was just about two years old, and feeding her dinner and then making a separate meal for my husband and I wasn't working. Even though I'm a dietitian, I never learned how to cook for a family. Yes, I could easily eat healthy between microwaving oatmeal, getting free lunch at work (which always included a big salad) and putting together a select few dinners. But cooking for a growing family was completely different territory, and to be honest, it scared me to death.

I decided to start cooking for my family by purchasing cookbooks, signing up for email newsletters and searching recipes online. In those early days, I made so many (now laughable) mistakes. I often chose recipes completely out of my league in terms of both the cooking skills and the time needed to prepare them. It was not uncommon for me to ask my husband to pick up Pollo Loco on the way home due to an epic meal failure. But slowly, I began to build some family favorites.

I came to depend heavily on meal planning: shopping on the weekend and planning the whole week's meals ahead of time. Although meal planning helped, I felt like it was just keeping me above water, and I was still struggling a lot of the time. I was especially frustrated that hardly any of the recipes I tried were sticking in terms of being added to my meal repertoire. When I asked my readers about this, they admitted that most cookbooks they purchased only yielded one or two "sticky" meals.

I started to question this recipe-centric strategy. I often read how chefs don't even follow recipes. They may develop them, use them for inspiration, but they don't rely on them at home. Yet here I was, stuck with a kitchen full of ingredients I only used once for *this* or *that* recipe. What I was doing clearly wasn't working. But how could I change it? I still wasn't sure.

My turning point came while talking to my friend's mom about how she did dinner when her kids were little. She described how she rotated a set number of meals: a fish dinner, a vegetarian meal, a meat dish. I realized that maybe family dinners happened more frequently back then because meals and planning were simpler. I looked at all the food ideas around me, seeing them as a hindrance for the first time. I no longer believed articles like "150 Ways to Make Chicken" were helping me in any way.

I also read about "decision fatigue," the tiring of one's mind due to the flood of daily choices. In other words, stressing over the little things like what to cook or what to wear every day steals energy from the big things like work, parenting and life! Did you know famous people like the president purposely wear the same outfit every day to save their brainpower for their important work? It makes complete sense when you think about it. Continually making small decisions from the time you get up to the time you go to bed is a significant brain drain.

I realized more of my time was spent agonizing over what to make than actually cooking. Decision fatigue and a lack of focus were the *real* reasons meal planning and cooking felt like such a monumental task. After connecting the dots, I made it my mission to simplify dinner. I stopped my subscription to cooking magazines and e-newsletters and gave away my unused cookbooks. Instead of making random recipes, I focused on the meals that already worked for my family while creating a vision for my family's table. I set out to master a month's worth of go-to dinners with the goal of rotating them on a daily basis.

I intuitively knew my kids would benefit from this simple way of planning and cooking. It just seemed like a better way to expose them to a variety of foods, teach them to cook and keep myself sane in the process. Yet even I was surprised how a meal rotation exceeded my expectations. This new way of "doing dinner" literally squashed the typical obstacles involved with feeding a family.

Allow me to show you what I mean.

Tackling Common Obstacles to Family Dinners

When I was in the beginning stages of writing this book, two high-profile articles about family dinner were published: "What if You Just Hate Making Dinner?" in *The New York Times Magazine* and "Let's Stop Idealizing the Home-Cooked Family Dinner" in *Slate*.[1,2] The first was written by a mom appalled that she's now expected to cook dinners, rebelling against the advice given in popular family cookbooks. And the second challenges the romanticized version of family dinners by highlighting key barriers like time, money and picky kids.

Many foodie parents got defensive about these articles, but I welcomed them for their honesty. Because without this type of honesty, we will never find solutions that work. The truth is cooking for children poses challenges that cooking without kids simply does not. I reached out to some of my blog readers to dig into the common barriers. Here are the top five themes that kept coming up.

1. Meal planning works in theory, but reality tells a different story. "I know in my head that doing a better job of planning meals ahead of time would streamline dinner," says Regina, "but I often don't think of dinner till about 2:00 p.m., when my twins are napping."

Tracie is a mom who doesn't mind cooking but says, "it's the idea of what to cook that is daunting some weeks. I menu plan and try and shop weekly for what we need, but sometimes I feel short on ideas to mix things up a bit and not have the same thing every week. Side dishes tend to be an afterthought."

Traditional meal planning wasn't working for me either. While I blamed myself when things went wrong, I can now see decision fatigue as the real culprit. It took a lot of energy to choose five weekly meals out of my big book of recipes. I thought switching to monthly meals would help, but it didn't (I just procrastinated even more!). I put off meal planning until a few minutes before shopping and often did a quick and sloppy job. Monday and Tuesday were usually good, but by Thursday I had no interest in making the dish I planned. My meal plan had a meager 50–60% success rate.

There were also gaps in my meals and side dishes that needed attention. Without a solid foundation of base recipes, planning meals was bound for failure. I address my process for solving this problem in Chapters 1–3. In short, by mastering a set number of meals and sides, meal planning took care of itself.

2. *I'm just not that into cooking.* Some people just don't enjoy cooking and all that goes with it. Even those who like to cook admit to the joy being compromised due to the busyness of family life. "I'm one who does like to cook, but I don't always like the drudgery of cooking dinner day in and day out," says Michelle. "It's just not as much fun as planning a fancy dinner party or baking up holiday treats. The fun goes out the window when you have to do it every single night."

But some admit to a hate/hate relationship with cooking. "I work full time and hate to cook. Not dislike; I actually despise it," says Lisa. "However, with a nine-year-old picky eater and a newborn, I know I need to do more to make healthier meals for my family. I am trying to find ways to make easy meals that I can still manage when I go back to work from maternity leave."

I used to dread every minute of cooking, but I started noticing glimpses of enjoyment piercing through. I noticed how I felt about cooking was directly related to the process and the final product. I think the key to cooking enjoyment is making it fit your personal style and life. This book details how I made dinner easier and enjoyable for my family and me. You might choose to do something differently, but I hope to inspire you to get more rewards out of the process.

3. *Complaining and picky kids kill cooking motivation.* The biggest obstacle facing parents is family members' different food preferences, especially kids'. "I do love the idea of family dinners, but the reality is that I end up spending an hour prepping and cooking something that my kids barely even want to taste," says Tammy. "Also, my husband very rarely gets home before the kids go to bed, so that leaves just me eating the meal that I've spent all this time on. It's no wonder it's difficult to motivate myself to cook each night."

Another mom shares a universal truth of cooking for children: "I enjoy cooking until the boys (age 10 and 12) realize what I am making because that is when the complaining begins," says Megan. "Even when I make stuff they like, there is always a comment on where I went wrong. The whining is a motivation killer."

I frequently write about picky eating, so that knowledge is sprinkled throughout this book. Even with this knowledge, I still found myself shying away from meals (and restaurants) to avoid hearing my kids complain and whine. The development of my meal vision and core meal rotation helped me commit to a wider variety of meals. I also better defined my "side strategy"—choosing sides my kids like when I'm not sure they will like the main meal—to give them exposure without all that pressure. Every family needs to have a list of dinner rules, including "No complaining allowed, please." These rules, and tips geared towards kids, are detailed in Chapter 4.

4. Time and schedule constraints make homemade meals next to impossible. Parents are busy these days, many living in dual-income households, resulting in limited time and energy for cooking. "I used to like cooking, and still do on the weekends, but the compressed schedule and craziness when I get home takes the fun out of it," says Kristen. "Not to mention, after bedtime I have to clean up and make lunches, which usually puts me at 9:00–9:30 p.m."

Most parents do not want to give up time with their kids for elaborate cooking. "As two full-time working parents, we don't want to sacrifice family time for complex recipes and tons of dishes to wash!" says Jen. "We need meals that are on the table (start to finish) within 30 minutes or less. Often recipes sound like they'll be quick and easy, but I underestimate the time it takes to prep the ingredients or other hidden time sucks."

Each family needs to carefully choose their meals to match the amount of time they are willing to spend on preparation and cooking. I work from home, so I prefer meals that allow me to prepare some of the meal earlier, pick up my kids and only have to make a few simple items come dinnertime. But someone who works away from home might need all-day slow-cooker meals or items that are easy to prep the night before for quick cooking after arriving home. I discuss how to pick the best meals in Chapter 3.

5. One meal with very young children? LOL! It can be tough when kids are really young, going to bed early or getting really clingy at dinnertime. "Family dinners are fairly nonexistent at my house right now," admits Regina. "My husband and I both work full time and have a one-year-old and a four-year-old. Usually, we feed the kids at night and then eat dinner ourselves once they are in bed."

It may not be possible to eat together every night with young children, but it's never too early to work on your family's meal vision with the goal of making one meal a night instead of two. Or, you can think out of the box like Erin did. "I bathe my kiddos before dinner, so my husband has a better chance of eating with us," she says. "I re-did our timeline, and we are so very happy I did."

In our house with a six- and nine-year-old, and a husband usually home on time, this isn't a problem, but I've been there before. The key is to do the best you can, feeling good that you are working towards eventual family dinners.

Why Bother with Family Meals? (How to Use This Book)

You don't need me to tell you the benefits of family meals. The problem isn't that people don't understand the importance of eating together, it's that the typical one-size-fits-all advice doesn't make getting meals on the table any easier. That's because individuals need to discover their own solutions. But for this to happen, there needs to be a mind shift about the whole process. This sentiment from one of my readers, Tawn, helps explain a universal truth about family meals that is important to acknowledge up front:

What I think is missing in a lot of the recent articles that received national attention is that we HAVE to eat. There is no way around the work, even if the "work" is going through the drive-through and then having to clean up the car (ugh, that smell!). The history of humanity has revolved around the need to eat and the ingenuity of the omnivore in solving it.

Whether we go through the drive-through, pick up packaged foods or cook food from scratch, we have to feed our families. It seems to me, if we are miserable the whole time we are doing it (or feel guilty about those choices), that severely compromises family connection and daily joy. Because what we resist persists, right? Why not embrace family cooking with a touch of gratitude, creativity and some optimism. We have an opportunity to create meals that taste wonderful, match our schedules and nourish our family's bodies. And when you think about it, we sure are lucky to live in a time where food is accessible and relatively inexpensive. No doubt about it, the initial process takes work, but once you get through the hard part, you can sit back and relax as described in the opening paragraph of this book.

Once I started looking at family meals in this new, more positive light, everything got better. This new mindset led me to a way of making family dinners enjoyable, relatively seamless (they will never be perfect) and nutritious. This book is about sharing my process with you while giving you strategies on how you can do the same thing, but in your own way.

My strategy is built around three S's: *Simplify, Strategize* and *Stop Agonizing.* Part 1: Simplify Your Meals is about developing laser focus. In Chapter 1, I show you how to sit down with your recipes and meals and identify what is working and let go of what isn't. Next, in Chapter 2, you'll apply this same principle to your kitchen. This not only gives you access to the food you use but also makes it easier to keep your kitchen stocked. In Chapter 3, I'll give you concrete ideas on how to create a meal vision, the meals you want to revamp and add to your meals that work. You can work off all of my examples, but yours will reflect your own preferences. Lastly, Chapter 4 includes the family dinner rules every parent needs to make eating with kids as pleasant and effective as possible. In Part 2: Strategize Your Meals, I get cooking, dividing chapters into five themes: Mexican, Italian, Square Meals, Asian and Greek Inspired and Seasonal. I show you how I developed meals and sides that work for my family along with simple strategies like meal short cuts, theme nights and assigning cooking jobs for my kids. If one of my recipes looks good to you, try it as is. Even better: tweak it to make it your own.

The third and last section, Part 3: Stop Agonizing over Family Dinners, is about getting your core meal rotation in place. This is the number of meals you will rotate for dinner on a regular basis. I chose 25 meals, making five per week. Yours might be less or more. With a rotation in place, you really can stop agonizing over what to cook for dinner. Instead, you can put your energy into making your rotation—and meals—even better. Chapter 11 includes ideas on how to start and modify your rotation over time. After all, your rotation is a work in progress as seasons change, meals lose their luster and new ones are needed to breathe in fresh air. The last chapter encourages you to take the leap of creating your own cookbook.

This approach works because it puts you in charge. It starts with you making a plan of what you want on your family's table. It's flexible, leaving room for growth and change over time. You make all the decisions in one fell swoop, so you can avoid the crippling effects of decision fatigue. It makes it infinitely easier to navigate the millions of recipes out there. Here are the key benefits a core meal rotation can bring to your family:

- Children get repeated exposure to food, which is what they need to eventually accept more items.
- You can be more thoughtful with your side strategy, making sure there is always at least one side kids accept, so you don't have to worry when they reject the main entrée.

- Meal preparation becomes simple, making it easier to have kids help with meals, even if it's a small job like rinsing beans or washing vegetables.

- Creating several "base" meals and sauces makes it easier to switch up ingredients like protein or vegetable sources. Research shows kids are more likely to accept food if it's in a familiar sauce.[3]

- Simplicity + repetition = always having ingredients on hand. No last-minute runs to the store or annoying calls to spouses or partners to pick up something on the way home.

- Shortcut strategies naturally flow from your rotation, like making sides ahead of time and creating spice mixes for quick preparation.

- It's ideal for family-style meal service, something that works great for everyone.

- No more taking time out of your relaxing weekend to plan a week's worth of meals; you can stop agonizing and enjoy!

I am especially grateful for the team of parents who reviewed this book before it was published. Throughout the book, you will see quotes and stories about how they used this information to make their family dinners more simple, effective and stress-free.

If you haven't already figured it out, I'm not your typical cookbook author. While most books focus on the *what* (recipes, nutrition info), I've always been fascinated with the *how*. In other words, I don't like offering advice on what to do, unless I feel someone has the right mindset and tools needed to utilize it. This cookbook is all about the *how* of family cooking. Because you can be given the most perfectly tested recipes—and meal plans—but the real challenge still remains: *figuring out how to do dinner in a way that works for your unique circumstances.* Mastering the *how* naturally makes the *what* (meals and recipes) much easier, fitting and sticky. I truly believe focusing on the how is the only way to crack the code on *What to Cook for Dinner (with Kids)*. When you've finished reading this book, I think you'll agree.

You don't need a million recipes to be a successful family cook. All you need is a streamlined list of meals that work for your family. Let's start by discovering what's working.

PART I: SIMPLIFY YOUR MEALS

"Simple can be harder than complex: You have to work hard to get your thinking clean to make it simple. But it's worth it in the end because once you get there, you can move mountains."

-Steve Jobs

1 DISCOVER WHAT WORKS AND WHAT DOESN'T

A few years into cooking, I realized there were some dinners I enjoyed cooking and others I dreaded. I found myself looking for excuses to make the meals I liked. This is typical with almost everything: we do what we enjoy and put off what we don't. Yet variety and exposure can suffer when making the same few meals over and over.

Sometimes the guilt would get to me, and I'd spend a week making anything but my favorite meals. You know, the meals I thought real family cooks *should* make. Then a huge light bulb went off. *My goal shouldn't be to make less of the meals I enjoy, it should be to create even more of them.* I pictured myself feeling good every time I went to cook. Feeling confident about variety, taste, nutrition and even my kids' eating. How amazing it would be, I thought, to enjoy cooking for my family most of the time.

My first step to revamping how I did meals was to let go of what wasn't working and focus on what was. Below is a list of supplies you will need for this chapter. Visit RaiseHealthyEaters.com/what-to-cook-for-dinner-templates to print out worksheets that will help you through the process (for Chapters 1-3) or use the Appendix.

- Three-ring binder (optional sheet protectors)
- Folder
- Access to all of your stored and printed recipes
- Cookbooks, magazines and other meal resources

Goodbye to Distracting Cookbooks, Newsletters and Magazines

Getting organized has been a lifelong challenge for me, but for the last year or so, I've started to see that a big part of the problem is that I have too much stuff to organize. Then I read *The Life-Changing Magic of Tidying Up* and was convinced this was THE problem.[4] In her best-selling book, Marie Kondo argues that even if we go through our stuff on a regular basis, we simply keep too much of it. Her solution is to go through each item and ask yourself one question: Does this spark joy?

Charlotte, a working mom, puts it this way: "I read an article where the author asked, 'has this outlived its usefulness?' I found that helpful because I could be okay with the fact that at one time, there may have been a reason to buy and have something, but that it may be time to part with it as it has indeed outlived its usefulness!"

I knew that many of my recipes and books had outlived their original purpose. So I started with my cookbooks, piling them all on the floor, picking up each one. When I touched and opened them I knew instantly whether it should stay or go. I gave most of them away but kept the select few that really excite me about cooking. This allows me to store my most cherished cookbooks in my kitchen, instead of stuffing all my cookbooks back in the closet.

For the time being, I decided my cooking magazines and recipe e-newsletters had to go. Maybe later I could subscribe to them, if I felt it was going to help my cooking goals. But while developing my rotation, I knew the constant influx of meals and recipes could too easily pull me off track.

Next, you'll want to go through all your recipes. I trusted my instincts and let go of the meals I just knew wouldn't work. If I was torn about it, say, I liked the meal idea but the recipe itself never worked, I put it in a separate folder (you will revisit this folder in Chapter 3). It was comforting to know that if I really wanted the recipe at a later date, I could look it up online.

The last and most important step is to pinpoint which recipes actually work for your family and *why*. Because if you can understand the why, you can create even more go-to dishes you love. And that's exactly what I did.

Putting What Works in One Place

I gathered all of my working recipes and organized them in a three-ring binder. By "working," I mean meals that I make regularly, are popular and fairly simple. I had to be honest with myself about this list. It's very important to only include your true go-to meals in your three-ring binder for a clear picture of what you have and like to cook. After doing this, I found I had about 12 meals I call my Tried and True meals. Here they are:

Tried and True Meals
1. Turkey tacos
2. Fish tacos
3. Quesadillas
4. Spaghetti and meatballs with homemade sauce
5. Shrimp linguine
6. Slow-cooker vegetarian lasagna
7. Slow-cooker Greek chicken pitas
8. Chicken enchiladas
9. Salmon or trout made three ways
10. Chicken or fish tenders/nuggets
11. Turkey chili
12. Slow-cooker white bean and ham soup

After going through this same process, Meghan discovered that out of 356 meals in her online recipe book, only 19 of them were Tried and True. Jen ended up deleting a few years' worth of recipes she had saved in her email account that she was going to try someday. "Simplicity is so freeing!" she says. "And it's nice to remember that being a good parent doesn't mean I have to make new, complex Pinterest-worthy dinners every night of the week!"

Cari realized she didn't have many Tried and True recipes. "I tend to try different things all of the time in an effort to find meals that are 'healthy' that satisfy my need to eat less gluten and my family's enjoyment of pasta and bread," she says. "I also want and like to eat a lot of vegetables, but my family doesn't, so it's hard to decide on those as well."

Examining the Why Behind What Works

With your Tried and True meals in front of you, think about why they work and why others don't. For me, I like meals with simple preparation. I especially like meals where at least part of the meal can be cooked in the slow cooker or that I can make earlier in the day. There are certain ingredients I enjoy cooking with, like garlic, beans, certain spices, lemon, veggies and vinegar. I'm fine with expanding my ingredient base, but I have learned that it's better to do so slowly, or else I end up with a bunch of ingredients I never use.

The most surprising thing I noticed is most of these recipes were mine. In other words, these were the meals I tweaked and modified over time to fit my cooking style and family's taste. For example, it took many tries of fish tacos to get it to Tried and True status. I scratched pan-frying (which I hate) for baking using my chicken tender breading. There were a couple of recipes I didn't change much from the original, but they were the exceptions.

"The meals that work for my family end up not only being easy to cook, but fun to cook together," says George. "The entrees also need to be easy to mix up with sides, so we can have the same entree multiple times in the week." Jen discovered she preferred simple meals that are quick to make or ones that can be doubled and frozen for later meals.

I consider a meal's popularity, but my kids do not have to accept something for me to include it in my Tried and True list. They are still learning about food, and I understand it takes time for them to accept certain dishes. While it's wonderful to have meals kids enjoy, and everyone needs some of those, it isn't one of my criteria for making the meal on a regular basis. This is true for my husband and me, too. There are certain meals we don't particularly love, but the kids enjoy them, so they are included.

Taking the time to figure out what is working *right now* gives you many clues into developing even more of these meals. When you are done with this chapter, you should have a three-ring binder with your Tried and True recipes, a folder with recipes you're not ready to give up on but aren't working for some reason, and your most treasured cooking resources. Before dreaming up new meals, your kitchen needs some serious attention.

2 STREAMLINE YOUR KITCHEN

I'm always put off with articles and books that offer advice on how to stock a kitchen. When I follow it, I end up with stuff I rarely use. One time, while trying to fish out a can of beans, I bypassed five unused canned items! I knew a good deal of what was in my kitchen just sat there taking up space. The next logical step after going through your recipes is to do the same with your kitchen.

You want to dive into your cabinets, fridge and freezer, assessing what's inside asking one very important question: *Do I actually use this?* Here's a step-by-step plan of how I did it.

Step 1: Make a list of what you want to stock. I jotted down the foods from my Tried and True list and the items my family eats for breakfast, lunch, snacks and dessert. I decided to keep these items stocked at all times. This mainly included nonperishable items like dry goods and somewhat-long-term perishable items like dairy and frozen foods. Fresh fruits and vegetables would be shopped for, stored and cleaned out on a weekly basis.

Step 2: Go through your cabinets. The first thing I did with my cabinets was toss past-date stuff. If it wasn't on my stock list from Step 1, I gave it away if it was still good. Even if it was something I thought I might use— unless pricey—I still gave it away (my philosophy is I can always buy it later when I will really need it). My goal was to only have on hand items I use with regularity. Of course, I would add new items as needed.

I analyzed my cookware as well. If I hadn't used a pot or pan in a very long time, I gave it away or tossed it if it was in very poor condition. If this is hard, you can store it in a box to revisit later. It's never easy to give away stuff, but the freedom it gives you is well worth it.

Step 3: Go through your fridge and freezer. The fridge should be gone through on a weekly basis. I went through each level and threw out what was old, paying close attention to all those condiments on the side. I tried to be brutal and keep only what I use. The three-year-old relish had to go!

The freezer is trickier because that stuff never goes bad; it only loses its quality over time. I arranged items by date, so I could use the older items first. The food I just knew I wasn't going to cook got tossed.

Steps 4: Make handy lists. Next, I made organized lists for food storage. Each night before my big shopping trip, I take an inventory like they do in restaurants. Weekends are reserved for quickie trips, usually for perishables items. This has helped me cut down on last-minute grocery stops and the dreaded call to hubby to pick up something on the way home, followed by the frustrating call of him not being able to find it. *(What do you mean you don't see it? It's right next to the enchilada sauce!)*

Step 5: Store food properly. To keep food waste down, I developed a comprehensive food storage list you can access at RaiseHealthyEaters.com/what-to-cook-for-dinner-templates. I list commonly used items and suggested storage times to help with spring cleaning and food safety. If you can't find something on my list, search online.

This is the ideal time to reorganize your kitchen the way you want it. I decided to sort food in the cabinet by food group—grains, protein, fruit and veggies, sweets and miscellaneous—instead of by snack food, canned items, etc. This helps teach my kids about how to put a balanced snack together, so it ends up being a nutrition lesson, too. My fridge is organized by level. Top is drinks, next is leftover items followed by dairy and grains. I have three drawers: one for fruit, one for veggies, and another for deli meat and cheeses.

When you are done, it will feel good to have a well-organized kitchen with easy access to the food you love to cook. Next up: creating a vision for what you want to see on your family's table.

3 CREATE YOUR MEAL VISION

After having children, things change in the food department. Most of us don't take the time to embrace this change and consider the type of meals that will work for the whole family. "Before we had a child, meals were planned based mostly on variety and 'wow' factor... that doesn't work now," says George. "We compromise on variety now to give the family more time around the table together and not in the kitchen."

Hopefully, examining what is currently working has got you thinking about new meals and sides that can fill in the blanks. With your Tried and True meal list in hand, and an organized kitchen, you can begin developing your vision for family dinners.

What Are Your Cooking Preferences?

First, you'll want to consider the type of meals you prefer in terms of cooking and nutrition. I strive for just enough variety of food, but too much overwhelms me. I've heard some food bloggers never repeat the same meal in a year. I also know people who can just work off what is in their kitchen and create great meals. If I tried to do either of these things, I would be stressed, and food would go to waste. I don't consider myself a natural cook, but I'm finding what works for me. I will occasionally make a more complicated meal, but aim for simple most of the time. I actually don't mind making more involved meals if I can do it ahead of time, so mealtime is not chaotic.

"For me, it's really about what the family will like and how easy it will be to prepare," says Charlotte. "Dishes with a long list of ingredients and complicated or messy preparation do not make the cut!"

Be honest with yourself about how many different meals you need, and your ideal cooking preferences, and you'll be better able to choose appropriate meals.

What is Important in Terms of Nutrition and Health?

You'll want to home in on health and nutrition. I aim for a Mediterranean-ish diet: think lots of olive oil, fruits, vegetables, whole grains, low-fat dairy (except cheese), nuts, beans, legumes, fish and lean meats. I will make the occasional high-fat meat, like carnitas (pork shoulder), but that's about it. I'm not a big fan of red meat but am open to making it. I try to get two fish meals per week, one dinner and one lunch. Although health is a key consideration, so is enjoyment. The meals in this book mirror my personal application of the nutritional science without being too rigid or restrictive.

Cari is focused on her athletic son's needs. "My son is an athlete and needs better nutrition," she says. "My latest interest is sports nutrition in young athletes, so I have been reading up on that and would like to incorporate meals that support him that will also be healthy."

Maybe there are food allergies or intolerances in your family, or, like Cari, you have active kids. Detailing what you need in terms of nutrition helps you choose the right meals.

Factor in Family Preferences

The last and maybe most important consideration is food preferences. I thought about each family member. My husband really enjoys meat, but when I ask if he wants more meals with meat his patent answer is "whatever is healthy." We occasionally go to In-N-Out Burger, and all I have to do is say, "In-N-Out," and he is dressed and out the door in minutes. Luckily, he loves beans and salads too. My nine-year-old daughter has turned into a protein gal! It's much easier to cook for her now because she likes chicken cooked most ways, and fish is her favorite. She's also my big fruit eater and is just warming up to salads. My six-year-old son is still pretty picky but he rarely complains about any meal. His favorite dinners are quesadillas, burritos, taco night, chicken pita (he only adds hummus, no chicken), macaroni and cheese, pizza, cheeseburgers (turkey or meat) and spaghetti with meatballs. Nobody in our house has food intolerances or allergies, and we all love sweets: chocolate and ice cream are our favorites.

Another consideration is the age and stage of growth of children in the house. Young children tend to like ingredients served separately, so I look for meals I can serve family-style, placing big bowls of food on the table to pass around, rather than pre-plating items. Older children may be more adventurous and involved in activities, so one-pot dishes can work great. I explain the sides and family-style service I choose for my family in each chapter.

My goal is to challenge my kids just enough while providing a safety net. If it's a new meal, I like to get a good side dish going to give them time to warm up. I also consider the gaps in their food exposure. Sometimes we are out and I realize they've never seen a type of food, and I think "that might be good to include in the rotation."

"When I look at new recipes, I'm usually trying to find one that he might be willing to try," says Jen, who mainly focuses on her son's preferences when planning meals. Katja points out: "I'd say a little of kids' preferences, but more of YOUR preferences;

27

you are cooking, and you want your kids to learn to like what you like to eat and cook!"

List your family's preferences and goals for children's eating, keeping them in mind as you pinpoint your meal vision.

Choose a Formula for Family Dinner

Charlotte lived in France at two different times, once with a child, and she had the opportunity to observe firsthand a very different attitude towards food and family meals. While there is a lot of variety in what they eat, meals are built around a basic formula: an appetizer (called an entrée) that can be a small plate of crudités, a slice of smoked salmon with lemon or a boiled egg with some mayo on top, a main dish that is often fish or a meat accompanied by either a starch or a vegetable, green salad, cheese or yogurt for the kids, and then dessert, which on weeknights is often fresh fruit. "The standard progression means that everyone—especially the kids—knows what to expect and that they are *expected* to take at least some of each course," she says. "I think the 'formula' makes it easy for the family cook to decide what to make, too!"

The French have a specific formula for meals, making it easier to plan and serve food. Your formula should fit you and your cooking style. It's important to think about the way you want to organize family dinners as you create your rotation. I detail my process of organizing meals in Part 3, but I just want to get you thinking about it now.

A key part of my formula for dinner meals is using theme nights. Mondays I serve Mexican. Tuesdays it's Italian. On Wednesdays, I let my children choose and make the meal, calling it "kids' choice" night (hubby works late). It has to be something easy as it provides me with a break from the usual dinner routine. Thursdays are either square meals (protein, veggie, etc.), an ethnic dish or grill night in the summer, and Fridays need to be something easy. I keep it flexible, though. If one of my kids has a late-afternoon activity, dinner is made in the slow cooker, or I choose something that needs little in the way of preparation.

Thinking more about it, Carey realized her most consistent meal-prep time was when she used theme nights. She had Mediterranean Monday, Taco Tuesday (but it was any Mexican dish), Whatever Wednesdays, Fish Fridays and Spaghetti Sundays (any Italian). Jen just looks at the calendar to see what fits, tweaking it during the week.

For every meal, I brainstorm a side strategy. Basically, these are familiar sides to share at the table to ensure kids have something to eat if they aren't ready to eat the main entree. For example, my daughter disliked tacos until she was about seven years old. I kept serving them with liked sides, and now she eats tacos. If you have young kids with plain tastes, over time they will tire of that plain food, their appetites increase, and they gradually partake in more and more meals. A side strategy is vital to this process.

The last part of my formula is to serve meals family-style instead of pre-plating food. Each part of the meal goes on the table in a dish and gets passed around for self-service. I encourage my kids to take each component, but the decision is ultimately theirs. I took advice from Kay Toomey, pediatric psychologist and developer of the family-centered Sequential Oral Sensory (SOS) approach to feeding, and incorporated a learning plate at dinnertime.[5] Basically, the food my children don't want on their plates goes on a small plate next to them so they can learn more about it by touching, looking or tasting if they want.

Here is my three-part formula for simplifying meals:

1. Theme nights based on food preferences and desired exposure
2. Predictable sides so kids know what to expect, which makes it less stressful when trying something new
3. Serving meals family-style by placing food in bowls so everyone can serve themselves

You don't have to do theme nights, but coming up with a formula for family dinner sure makes planning and execution easier.

Putting It All Together to Come Up with the Meals

With all of this in mind, it's time to brainstorm the types of meals and sides you want for your family meals. What classic meals are you not making but want to? For instance, I had a lasagna meal but not a Tried and True stir-fry recipe. I considered what was missing in terms of nutritional variety. I had some fish meals but needed more. I also needed more whole-grain sides and certain veggies were missing. "I definitely need more fish meals, and I want to add seasonal meals as a theme night," says Jen. "Plus, I am seriously lacking on side dish ideas; they're always an afterthought for me."

I went back to my folder of recipes from Chapter 1 that didn't make the Tried and True cut. Could I change anything to make them better? After going through this process, I came up with two additional categories of meals: In Between and Want to Make. The Tried and True meals are the ones you make easily. The In Between meals are either meals you used to make but stopped for some reason or they need work to reach Tried and True status. And last are the meals you want to get in the rotation for better variety, exposure and family food preferences. The list below is where I ended up after going through this process (meals were for winter, so the list includes soups and stews).

In Between Meals
Slow-cooker chicken teriyaki (almost there)
Thin crust pizza (I will do it!)
Base stir-fry (I haven't perfected the sauce)
Lentil casserole (I used to make and love)

Shrimp and broccoli bake (I make it differently each time)
Black bean and sweet potato burgers (needs more oomph)
Salmon cakes (I love the idea, but the results have been
disappointing)
Lentil soup (I can't settle on one recipe)
Slow-cooker Italian chicken with white beans (I used to make
and love)
Chicken or shrimp fajitas (the current recipe is too involved)

Want to Make Meals
Base Alfredo sauce with pasta and an alternate protein source
Slow-cooker curry (lentil or chicken)
Pork tenderloin
Tuna casserole (modern version without canned soup)
Meatloaf
Veggie soup (to use up veggies at the end of the week)
Butternut squash soup
Veggie frittata or crustless quiche

I also noted missing sides including mashed potatoes, green beans,
a whole-grain base side and a few grilled side dishes.

Cari's In Between meals included recipes she used to make
but hadn't had in awhile. Her Want to Make list mainly consisted
of how to include more grains that don't include gluten and more
vegetarian options. Once you get to work on these meals, some will
get scratched, and new ones may come into the mix. I know my list
never felt perfect, but that's okay. I had some occasional and
seasonal meals not included. The important thing was I finally had
a workable plan! I was becoming purposeful with my cooking, and
it felt really good.

It can be a little mind boggling, but formalizing what you
want to see on your family's table is a vital step. By now, in
addition to your Tried and True meals, you have a list of In
Between and Want to Make meals. Before you get cooking, let's
touch on the rules that make family dinners work.

4 INCORPORATE SANITY-SAVING FAMILY DINNER RULES

On my blog, Raise Healthy Eaters, and in my books, *Fearless Feeding* and *From Picky to Powerful*, I discuss research-based ways to feed kids to help them grow into good eaters. Feeding should be simple and works best when it is. Being consistent and straightforward with children about expectations at the table makes a world of difference.

In addition to creating meals that work, you also need some dinner rules to which you can refer when behavior gets out of line. Also, these rules help you commit to family meals. You can print them out at RaiseHealthyEaters.com/what-to-cook-for-dinner-templates. Post these rules on your fridge or, if you want something different, make your own.

1. You don't have to eat (but please join us at the table for family time).
Ellyn Satter's Division of Responsibility (DOR) is the key to avoiding power struggles at the table.[6] It's the feeding philosophy supported by most major health organizations like the American Academy of Pediatrics. DOR comes down to this: parents and kids are responsible for two very different jobs in the feeding realm. The parents' job is to choose the meals, when they will be eaten and where. Children are in charge of deciding whether or not they eat. Super simple.

If feeding goes awry, it's usually because a child is trying to take over the parent's job or the parent is pressuring kids to eat a certain way. Peace—and better long-term eating and food regulation—comes from keeping these jobs separate.

Some kids may do okay with small pushes and encouragement to try food, such as "one-bite" rules, but other kids view this as pressure, making mealtime a power struggle. Decide what is best for your family, but keeping DOR the anchor of your table will make the whole process enjoyable.

2. There will always be something at the table that you like. When a child comes to a table and sees a bunch of unfamiliar food, it can cause him to panic. I tell my kids that there will always put something on the table that they like. This helps for other reasons, too. Parents often complain that their kids say they are full, when in reality they didn't like the meal. Then, a half an hour later they are asking for snacks. Having something at the table children can fill up on avoids this very common problem.

You may worry that your child will never expand his food horizons but he will. After awhile, children tire of favorite foods, appetites increase and minds become less resistant. Continual exposure and offering with a safety net allows kids to expand at a pace that is right for them. If you think your child's picky eating may be out of the norm, my book *From Picky to Powerful* can help you decide if he needs an evaluation.

I also try to modify meals to help increase my kids' acceptance, as long as it's not too much trouble. For example, I always make two chicken enchiladas without sauce for my daughter. I used to keep the red pasta sauce off her meatballs, and now she eats the sauce (one day she just asked: "can I have sauce please?"). Throughout this book, I note these modifications along with my side strategy to give you some ideas.

Write down the meals your kids like and other foods you can serve as sides. Try to aim for a kid's favorite entree at least once a week, or make one night "kids' choice," so they can choose.

Having meals they love in the rotation (not every night), helps a great deal.

3. Helpers are appreciated! You will be assigned one small job before dinner.
Having kids help in the kitchen is good for a variety of reasons: from learning cooking skills to getting food exposure to lightening the load of parents. I find that posing the question, "Do you want to help make X?" rarely piques my kids' interest, so I've started assigning small jobs. Sometimes this is cooking or prep related to that night's meal and other times it's just setting the table.

In Chapters 5–10, I provide ideas for cooking jobs such as boiling water, washing veggies and sautéing meat or vegetables.

4. No food complaining allowed, please. I don't allow complaining at the table like "gross," "yucky" or "not this again." This rule is in place out of respect for the cook and others who do enjoy the food. I encourage my kids to simply say "No, thank you."

I don't punish my kids when they complain; I simply remind them of the rule and empathize, "It sounds like you're disappointed with the meal choice. Remember, no complaining, it's disrespectful to the cook."

As mentioned earlier, I serve dinner family-style, placing food in bowls and passing them around, allowing family members to serve themselves. I encourage my kids to take a bit of everything, even if they don't want to eat it. I remind them they are learning about food, and dinner is prime learning time.

5. No throwing food, but you can touch, smell and lick any part of your meal.
This one is geared towards younger kids who begin to throw food as they learn cause and effect: "If I throw this meatball, it falls to the ground and mom yells!" It's important for children to learn throwing food is not acceptable, but touching and getting to know your food should be allowed, as it helps children learn about the food's properties. Even with a six- and nine-year-old, I encourage them to gather as much information about a new food as they can

and touching is always the first step.

6. When you are done eating, that's it until breakfast, so make sure you fill your belly. After dinner (or sometimes dessert) is done, eating is also done. My kids understand this and rarely ask for food after dinner. Babies and toddlers may need a nighttime snack, but as kids get older, this is usually phased out. You don't want children holding out for after-dinner snacks.

7. When you are done eating, bring your plate to the sink. Having children bring their plate up to the sink not only helps with clean up, but it signals the meal is done. If they want to clear more plates, by all means, let them.

"After incorporating these rules, we have really changed our attitude (as the parents) about how much our son does (or, usually, doesn't) eat at dinnertime," says Meghan. "I don't think that he is necessarily trying more things yet, but I do know that dinner is no longer a stressful event. We spend a lot more time talking about the day than arguing over food."

Enforced family mealtime rules help keep dinners running smoothly. If things start getting off track, revisit this list to see where improvements need to be made. Or better yet, post it on the fridge for all to see.

Now it's time to move onto the next section, where you create the meals you will love to make and love to eat.

PART 2: STRATEGIZE YOUR COOKING

"In real life, strategy is actually very straightforward. You pick a general direction and you implement like hell."

-Jack Welch

5 FINDING INSPIRATION

Before I started my meal rotation, I was drowning in meal ideas. I received weekly recipes from cooking websites and followed food blogs. I subscribed to cooking magazines and also flipped through my mother-in-law's cooking magazines every Sunday, taking pictures with my phone. I had a computer file with a running list of Want to Make recipes and a three-ring binder chock-full of printed recipes, most of which I rarely made.

Now, I can see that too many choices were distracting me. It's kind of like when you sit down to do something on your computer, and you get an email that a friend tagged you on Facebook, so you go see that photo (secretly hoping it's not heinous). You check your timeline and see interesting articles and start reading them. You notice 30 minutes zipped by, and you try to get started on your original task, but as you turn to your homepage, you notice a piece of news you have to read. Now 45 minutes have gone by!

Searching for recipes this time was a much more focused effort. I really thought about what I wanted and wrote down my goals. Here's the difference between how I searched for recipes before and what I do now:

Before:
Try random recipes that look good → it is either a success or not (mostly not) → keep the recipe in a binder or save online (whether

it worked or not) → create a big binder of recipes, few of which I use → try to meal plan but end up making the same old meals

Now:
Decide which recipes I need → consider my cooking and family's preferences while searching → try or modify a recipe until I get it the way I want it → only store recipes I use → create a big binder of recipes I use and love → rotate a good variety of meals

Armed with your new clarity and plan, you just need to find some cooking inspiration.

Where to Start

To be held accountable, I ran a 30 Meals in 30 Days Challenge on my blog, making all the meals on my list and posting about them. Not only did it take over 30 days to finish, I kept tweaking and trying recipes after the series ended. Odds are, this process will take quite a bit of time for you, too, depending on your starting point.

I started with those In Between meals on my list. First, I tried to figure out why I didn't make these meals more often. For example, I realized I didn't care for either of the recipes I had for lentil soup. One recipe took too much time to prepare, and the slow-cooker recipe resulted in overcooked, mushy lentils. I searched online to see what other ingredients and preparation methods people use. Thinking of my preferred ingredients (but open to trying maybe one new one), and my cooking preferences, I came up with my tweaked recipe. The first time I did this with lentil soup, it turned out great. It often takes more tries, but sometimes I get lucky.

When it comes to the meals on my Want to Make list, I start with a favorite food blogger or website. If I'm trying to lighten up a comfort food, for example, I search the Meal Makeover Moms or Cooking Light's website. I also like All Recipes because they have so many reviews with modification ideas.

Of course, cookbooks are good sources, too. I go to the index of my favorite cookbooks to see if they have what I'm looking for. In some cases, if the recipe looks good as-is, I won't make any changes. But more often than not, I start by making small modifications. Other times, I make it completely on my own the first time going in a totally different direction than any recipe I find (I'm such a rebel!).

My readers have their own preferences when searching for recipes. Charlotte, loves reading cooking magazines for inspiration, and says "Pinterest can be helpful too, although you can get caught on some rabbit trails with all the new suggestions it brings up!" Jen also likes Pinterest, but admits that "it really drives me insane!" Because Meghan joined a CSA (community supported agriculture) for the first time, she's been using blogs, like Simple Seasonal, that focus on CSA and seasonal meals. Katja suggests learning to cook from what your own mom cooked and modify as needed.

No matter where you go looking for inspiration, just be careful not to overwhelm yourself, or it could backfire.

When to Give Up or Keep Working

Instead of trying out a brand-new recipe on a busy weeknight, I prefer to test new meals when my kids are at school or on the weekend. I save leftovers for lunches, so there is no waste. If it's a small change to a current recipe or a really straightforward new meal, I will make it for family dinner. The important thing is finding a recipe-testing method that works for you.

There are always a few meal ideas that are especially challenging to master no matter how hard you try. I almost gave up on a homemade thin-crust pizza, but instead I tabled it. After some time, and researching online, I figured it out! Even my husband was surprised I pulled it off after all the pizza crust disasters I put the family through. Other times, I realize it makes more sense to throw in the towel and search for a good brand or restaurant to get the job done. Most often, I just need a break and can come back at a later date with fresh eyes.

Sometimes the reason meals don't turn out has more to do with cooking methods than ingredients. For example, I easily screw up pan-frying, so I usually try to bake instead. You will see from my meals in this section that there is a story behind each one. Some just kind of evolved over time, others I got right on the first try, while others remain a struggle. When you are able to add another Tried and True recipe to the mix, the pain it took to get there just kind of fades away.

A Word on Recipe Sources

Most cookbooks contain recipes that were developed specifically for that book. This book is more about the process of how to simplify and strategize dinners. An important part of that process is successfully finding recipes and meal ideas from a variety of sources. Although a good amount of the recipes in this book are mine, others are adapted or originate from some very talented people. I always give credit for these recipes. In the cases where I don't provide the full recipe, I add a link to where you can find it online in the Notes section. I also provide links for adapted and inspired recipes.

Here are the places I go most often to find recipes or get cooking help:

You Tube (mostly for learning a cooking skill)
The Kitchn (cooking advice)
All Recipes
Food Network (Ellie Krieger, RD)
Food.com
Cooking Light
Mom's Kitchen Handbook

Super Healthy Kids
Meal Makeover Moms
Pioneer Woman
Wannabite
Weekly Bite
Budget Bytes
Damn Delicious
Weelicious
A Year of Slow Cooking
Simply Recipes
Asian Grandmother's Cookbook

Really, there's no shortage of inspiration out there—from cookbooks to blogs to magazines. Deciding your specific strategy for finding new meals will streamline the process. Sooner rather than later, though, you'll want to get cooking. Let's do it!

6 MEXICAN MEALS

Being from Southern California, I basically grew up on authentic Mexican cuisine. I remember getting money from my parents and walking to the local taco shop to buy taquitos. Now as an adult, "Health Mex" is by far my favorite genre of meals to eat and make. I love it all—salsa, beans and chips. Healthy Mexican is all about choosing simple cooking methods and ingredients for nutritious meals. In other words, you don't have to cook with lard or fry anything to make it taste great.

I think that's why I have Mexican meals planned for Monday. Also, Mexican Monday just sounds better than Taco Tuesday.

Secret Staples

To make Mexican night go smoothly, I have mastered a few key staples that I serve frequently. These are worth the time investment to get them the way you want them.

Taco Seasoning Mix

I throw my homemade taco seasoning mix in everything from beans to marinades and Mexican sauce. This saves lots of time measuring out spices while cooking. When I find myself getting

low, I stock back up and keep it in an old cleaned-out spice jar.
You can double or even triple the recipe. Please modify to fit your
family's preferences.

Ingredients:

- 2 Tbsp. chili powder
- 1 Tbsp. cumin
- 1 Tbsp. garlic powder
- 2 tsp. onion powder
- 1 tsp. salt

Directions:

1. Put all the ingredients in a small jar and shake well. Double or
triple the recipe if you prefer to make a larger batch.

Salsa

The next staple I have around at all times is a really good salsa. I
have been making The Pioneer Woman's Restaurant-Style Salsa for
a few years.[7] I love adding it to guacamole, taco meat, and topping
it on eggs or any Mexican dish. I make it once a month and freeze
half of it and leave the other half in the fridge for two weeks (then
replace it with the frozen half).

Pico de Gallo

It's also nice to have a pico de gallo-type of salsa you can put out
with meals to fill in tacos or just eat as a side. Here's my simple mix
to boost the flavor of any Mexican meal. Leftovers are great on
scrambled eggs the next day.

Ingredients:

- 4 tomatoes (Roma), chopped
- ¼ cup chopped onion

- ½ jalapeno pepper (seeds removed), chopped
- ½ cup minced cilantro
- 1 garlic clove, minced
- ¼ tsp. salt
- ½ lime, juiced
- pepper, to taste

Directions:
1. In a small bowl, combine tomatoes, onion, jalapeno, cilantro, garlic, salt, lime juice, and pepper. Mix with a spoon and serve. If you prefer, use a food processer to chop the veggies.

Guacamole

Some people like to add cilantro and tomatoes and even cheese to their guacamole, but I prefer this simple ingredient combo. Double or triple the recipe for a bigger crowd.

Ingredients:
- 1 medium avocado
- 1 Tbsp. low-fat plain yogurt
- 1 Tbsp. salsa
- salt, to taste
- lime juice (from a small squeeze of lime)

Directions:
1. Remove the avocado pit, spoon the avocado into a small bowl and mash with yogurt and salsa. Add salt to taste and a just a bit of lime.

Secret White Sauce

The final staple is what I call white taco sauce. This works well on quesadillas, in burritos and with fish tacos. It's super easy!

Ingredients:
- ½ cup plain low-fat yogurt
- ½ tsp. taco seasoning mix
- ½ lime, juiced

Directions:
1. In a small dish, mix yogurt, taco seasoning and lime juice.

Side Strategy

When serving Mexican food, my side strategy is to put out tortillas, cheese, beans and guacamole, so my kids can make a burrito if they want. I put it all out on the table and pass everything around. Think about the types of Mexican food your child eats. Maybe you always put out rice, fruit or something else that can go with the meal. That way you can relax, knowing your child will get fed *and* the exposure they need to eventually accept more items. Listed below are some side-dish recipes I regularly serve.

Spanish Rice

I never made Spanish rice until I watched my daughter chow down on it at a Mexican restaurant. I came up with this combo for my book *Fearless Feeding.* The key to good Spanish rice is browning the rice in some oil first. I like to make a big batch and freeze it to simplify Monday meals. I've tried it with brown rice, but it doesn't turn out the same. Meghan did some things differently, like using instant brown rice and swapping tomato paste for tomato sauce. Her three-year-old loved it!

Serves: 4-6

Ingredients

- 1 cup long-grain rice
- 2 Tbsp. olive oil
- ½ cup chopped onion
- 2 garlic cloves, minced
- 2 cups chicken broth (check cooking instructions on rice to adjust liquid as needed)
- 1 ½ Tbsp. tomato paste
- ½ tsp. salt

Directions:

1. In a medium sauce pan over medium-high heat, sauté rice in oil until lightly browned.

2. Add onion and sauté an additional 5 minutes. Add garlic for the last minute of cooking time.

3. Add broth, tomato paste and salt and mix until combined. Once the mixture comes to a boil, turn down the heat to low, cover, and simmer for about 25 minutes or until the rice absorbs the liquid.

Quickie Black Beans

Black beans are my favorite Mexican side dish, and I make them every week. I also use this simple recipe to make bean burritos on a busy Saturday. I use canned beans because I always have them on hand, but you could also cook dried beans in big batches and freeze them.

Serves: 4

Ingredients:

- 1 15-oz can black beans
- 1 Tbsp. olive oil
- 2 garlic cloves, minced
- ¼ cup broth

- 1 Tbsp. taco seasoning mix or cumin (or half Tbsp. each)
- ¼ tsp. salt

Directions:
1. Drain and rinse beans. Put oil and garlic in a small pot over medium heat. Once the garlic sizzles, add the beans, broth, seasoning and salt. Once it begins to boil, set aside until ready to serve.

Pinto Beans

I've tried pinto beans in the slow cooker many times but they are still hard after 8-10 hours! After some experimentation, I realized cooking them over the stove works better. I also discovered that pinto beans don't need a lot of spices added to them. Sometimes I add green peppers and onions to jazz them up. The leftovers can be used to make bean and cheese burritos or served with eggs in the morning.

Serves: 6-8

Ingredients:

- 1 pound dried pinto beans
- water
- 1 bay leaf
- 3 garlic cloves, minced
- ⅓ cup olive oil
- ½ tsp. crushed red pepper (or more if you prefer)
- 15 cranks of fresh ground pepper
- 1 tsp. salt (or more to taste)

Directions:

1. Rinse and sort beans in a colander and add them to a large stock pot with the bay leaf and cover with about an inch of water. Turn to medium-high heat until the beans boil and then turn down the heat a bit. Keep the beans cooking on medium heat for about two hours, frequently adding more water as it is absorbed.

2. After the beans have been cooking two hours, put olive oil and garlic in a small pan and cook on low for about 10 minutes. Add the oil and garlic mixture, red pepper and fresh ground pepper to the beans and stir. Partially cover and cook on low for 1-2 more hours or until beans are soft. Keep adding water as needed.

4. When the beans are done, remove the bay leaf and add salt. Mash for refried beans or eat whole.

Main Dishes

I include five Mexican dishes in my rotation at any one time, but some of my meals never make it in. For example, I make carnitas with pork shoulder in the slow cooker when entertaining and for special occasions. There are other meals I've tried that never stuck, like Mexican lasagna. Think about the Mexican food you like to make and build on it. Here are the meals I came up with (and their stories).

Turkey Tacos

I can't believe for years I used store-bought taco seasoning mix when making tacos. After having kids, I made the Meal Makeover Moms' Have-It-Your-Way Tacos recipe, which includes beans in the meat with garlic powder and cumin.[8] I realized my daughter (not a natural taco fan) was more likely to eat a taco if the beans and meat were separated, so I started cooking the meat separately. I eventually came up with my own taco seasoning mix mentioned earlier in the chapter.

This is a fun meal where every family members can make their own taco or burrito. I put out whole-wheat flour and corn tortillas. Of course, you can use another type of ground meat or a vegetarian option when making tacos.

Serves: 4-6

Ingredients:
- 1 pound ground turkey or other meat (or vegetarian) option
- 2 Tbsp. taco seasoning mix
- ⅓ cup salsa (I use the Pioneer Woman's restaurant-style salsa)

Directions:
1. Spray a sauté pan with cooking spray and heat it over medium to high heat. Add the meat and stir until it is cooked through. Drain any fat.
2. Add the taco seasoning mix and salsa and stir until well combined.
3. Serve with tortillas and any toppings such as tomatoes, pico de gallo, lettuce, peppers, cheese and guacamole.

Baked Burritos

My friend Marisa gave me this recipe years ago, and it's another quick way to use taco meat. It's one of these great make-ahead meals you can pop in the oven while helping with homework or attending to kids' needs. If your kids aren't into sauce, try making a few burritos without it.

Meghan made this meal, and her husband loved it. She said that next time, she will add half the sauce to the meat mixture and pour the other half on top. Also, she made the burritos the night before and stored the casserole dish in the fridge.

Serves: 4-6

Ingredients:

- 1 tsp. olive oil or cooking spray
- 1 pound ground turkey
- 1 15-oz can pinto beans
- 2 small cans (or 1 large) green chili enchilada sauce
- 1 onion, diced
- 2 garlic cloves, minced
- 1 tsp. cumin
- 2 tsp. chili powder
- large flour tortillas
- grated Monterey Jack cheese, cheddar or Mexican blend

Directions:

1. Preheat oven to 300°F (or 400°F if you made the burritos ahead of time). Brown the ground meat in a frying pan with a small amount of oil or cooking spray. Add the diced onion, garlic and spices. Simmer until well done.
2. Add the beans and stir. Fill each tortilla with meat mixture and fold into a burrito then place in a large casserole or roasting dish. Repeat until meat and bean mixture are all gone.
3. Cover with the green chili sauce and sprinkle with cheese. Place in the oven for about 15 minutes or until the cheese melts. If you premade the meal, cook at 400 for 20 minutes.

Fish Tacos

Getting to a fish taco recipe I loved was not easy. I tried so many recipes without success, I'm really surprised I never gave up. The problem is most recipes call for pan-frying fish, and I just couldn't make it work (it always stuck to the pan, and the whole processes stressed me out!). Once I decided to bake the fish and use the same breading mix I use for my chicken tenders, I had a keeper. I serve fish tacos with corn tortillas, shredded cabbage, white taco sauce, cheese, guacamole and salsa.

Serves: 4–6

Ingredients:
- ¾ cup bread crumbs
- ¼ cup Parmesan cheese, finely grated
- 2 tsp. breading mix (¼ tsp. each salt, paprika, mustard seed and garlic powder)
- 1 pound tilapia fillets, cut into 1-inch pieces
- ¼ cup melted butter or 1 beaten egg

Directions:
1. Preheat oven to 425°F. Top a cookie sheet pan with tin foil and spray with cooking spray.
2. Mix the first three ingredients in a bowl. Melt the butter or beat an egg in a separate bowl.
3. Dip the fish pieces into the butter or egg and then dredge them through the breading mix. Place the fish in lines on the foiled pan.
4. Bake for 15 minutes or until browned. If you like crispy fish, place the pan under the broiler for the last minute of cooking. Serve with shredded cabbage, white taco sauce, tomatoes, cheese and corn tortillas or taco shells.

Chicken Enchiladas

I'm not sure where the idea for this recipe originally came from, but I have been making it on and off for years. I've attempted a couple other chicken enchilada recipes, but they seem so involved. I asked my sister how she makes chicken enchiladas, and she lost me at, "I start by boiling the peppers." The thing is, my kids aren't really into this one yet. My daughter says the sauce is "too creamy," so I make a couple enchiladas with less sauce and no cheese topping. My son usually goes for the side options at the table. This meal goes wonderfully with black beans.

You can also change this up by substituting both the taco and red enchilada sauce with green chili sauce. When I do this, I add some cheese along with the chicken inside each tortilla.

Serves: 4–6

Ingredients
- 1 pound chicken breasts or tenders
- 4 oz light cream cheese (half an 8-oz container)
- 1 10-oz can red enchilada sauce
- 1 small onion, chopped
- 1 red bell pepper, chopped (optional)
- 5–6 large whole-wheat flour tortillas (you can also use smaller ones)
- taco sauce (mild or not — your choice!)
- 1–2 cups shredded cheddar cheese or Mexican cheese blend

Directions:
1. Spray a skillet or pan with cooking spray and turn on to medium high heat. Place chicken in pan, turning frequently. While cooking, take a fork and knife and shred the chicken while it cooks. Continue this until meat is shredded and cooked through.
2. Preheat the oven to 350°F. Add the chopped onion, red pepper, cream cheese and enchilada sauce to the chicken and stir to combine. After the mixture starts boiling, turn off the heat and set aside.
3. Spray a 9x13-inch baking pan with cooking spray. Fill the tortillas with the chicken mixture and fold each side over. I usually get 5–6 big enchiladas and then make a couple small ones for the kids. Cover with as much taco sauce as desired and top with the cheese.
4. Cover with foil and cook in the oven for 20 minutes. Remove the foil and cook uncovered for an additional 5–10 minutes or until

cheese is completely melted.

Black Bean and Chicken Quesadillas

I knew these quesadillas would go into the rotation because they have been a favorite go-to meal for a while now. I love quesadillas because they are easy to change up. Kids can make their own from ingredients you have laid out. It's a great low-maintenance finger food you can serve with guacamole, salsa and some fruit.

I make these with my favorite Trader Joe's whole wheat and olive oil wraps. Most store-bought tortillas have what seem to be an endless list of ingredients, but these are so simple—and made with olive oil! Kids may want to start by only adding cheese, and that's fine. Through the years, you will see them beef up their quesadillas. Right now, my kids will take beans, cheese and some chicken.

Serves: 2-4

Ingredients:

- whole-wheat tortillas
- Mexican cheese blend
- ½ pound cooked chicken, chopped
- ½ 15-ounce can black beans
- 1 tsp. oil
- 2 tsp. taco seasoning mix
- Large tomato, chopped
- ¼ red onion, sliced
- white taco sauce (pg. 29)

Directions:

1. Rinse the beans and put about half of them in a small bowl. Mix in oil and taco seasoning mix. Roughly mash with a fork.
2. Put out the cooked, chopped chicken and the rest of the toppings.

3. Spread the bean mixture on the bottom of a tortilla and layer with chicken, tomatoes, onions, drips of white taco sauce and cheese. Top with another tortilla. If making small quesadillas, only fill toppings on half the tortilla and fold.
4. Spray a large sauce pan with cooking spray or butter. Cook each quesadilla on medium heat until browned on both sides and the cheese melts. Serve with guacamole and salsa.

Mexican Fiesta Bowl

In the summertime, it's nice to have a grill option for Mexican Mondays. We use this marinade to grill chicken or shrimp.

Serves: 4

Ingredients:
- 1- 1 ½ pounds chicken or shrimp
- ¼ cup olive oil
- ¼ cup lime juice
- 3 garlic cloves, minced
- 1½ tsp. taco seasoning mix
- ½ tsp. salt

Directions:
1. If using chicken breasts, cut large portions in half and/or pound thin with a mallet between two sheets of plastic wrap until it's about ½-inch thick. This helps the chicken cook evenly and quickly.
2. In a medium bowl, mix the olive oil, lime juice, garlic, taco mix and salt. Add chicken or shrimp to the bowl or place both marinade and protein in a large plastic bag. Marinade chicken or shrimp one or more hours before grilling.
3. Grill chicken on medium-high heat for 3-4 minutes per side or until the internal temperature reaches 165°F (if you do not pound

thin the chicken it will need to be cooked longer). Cook shrimp on high heat for 5-6 minutes turning throughout.

4. Serve the protein with beans, tomatoes, cheese, greens, salsa and avocado and let everyone make their own bowl.

Cooking Jobs for Kids

A key advantage of rotating meals is that preparation becomes very familiar. This makes it easier to give kitchen jobs to kids, so they can gradually learn how to cook. Younger kids need more assistance, but as kids get older, they can really help out.

Carey says that she is having her kids help in the kitchen more and more. "I'm even getting more adventurous and allowing them to use knives," she says. "I always try to keep things loose and my expectations low about a possible mess, something taking longer to do, or someone needing to leave before the task is done."

Young, beginner cooks (five years old and under) can:
- Measure ingredients
- Rinse and drain beans
- Stir during sauté with assistance
- Mix and mash avocadoes when making guacamole

Older, more experienced cooks (six years old and over) can:
- Make simple sauces and marinades
- Make guacamole and white sauce
- Chop veggies (assist as needed)
- Follow simple recipes (practice doing it together, then observe while they try)

Goals

Right now, I'm pretty content with my Mexican dishes. In the future, I would like to try a tostada night. As my kids get older, I wouldn't mind incorporating more one-pot dishes, like a good enchilada casserole. I may even try Mexican lasagna again.

I hope this has given you some good ideas on how to pull together Mexican night. Let's move on to Italian.

7 ITALIAN MEALS

I think Italian is one of the easiest family meals to cook, and it is certainly kid friendly. What makes it even easier is strategizing some good base sauces. I've worked through many failures to come up with a homemade red sauce, a lighter Alfredo-like white sauce and a garlic olive-oil sauce; they work for us and my cooking style. When you have these base sauces, it's easier to switch out vegetables and protein sources. Get your kid loving a sauce, and use it to introduce a new food. Let's dig right in, starting with my secret staples.

Secret Staples

Having a few staples for Italian dinners is a lifesaver. Here's what I keep on hand at all times.

Italian Seasoning Mix

My first staple is an Italian seasoning mix I have on hand for various dishes. You can also buy Italian seasoning, but finding the right mixture can enhance cooking. I leave salt out of my mix, so I can add as much as I want during cooking. After experimenting with different spices, this is what I have come up with:

Ingredients:

- 1 Tbsp. basil
- 1 Tbsp. oregano
- ½ Tbsp. marjoram
- ½ Tbsp. thyme
- ½ Tbsp. rosemary
- 2 tsp. garlic powder
- 1 tsp. red pepper

Directions:

1. Put all the ingredients in a small jar and shake well. Double or triple the recipe if you prefer larger batches.

Homemade Marinara Sauce

Next is a versatile marinara sauce. It's understandable if you want to stick with a favorite jarred sauce, but I think it's worth coming up with on a homemade sauce you can make ahead and freeze. I was stuck on the idea of adding in all these extra vegetables, but it comprised both the taste and look (think: orange!), so I decided it wasn't for me, even though the kids ate it. This recipe makes about 1½ jars, so I double it to make three, which gets me through the month. You can also add meat and freeze it, but I like to keep the sauce plain, so I have the option of adding meat or making meatballs separately.

Serves: 6

Ingredients:

- 2 Tbsp. olive oil
- 1 cup chopped onion
- 4–5 garlic cloves, minced
- 1 large carrot, grated (or two small carrots)
- 3 tsp. Italian seasoning mix

- 1 bay leaf
- ½ tsp. salt
- ½ tsp. sugar
- 15 cranks freshly ground pepper
- 1 large 28-oz can tomato pureed or whole tomatoes
- 1 15-oz can tomato sauce
- 1 6-oz ounce can tomato paste
- 1 cup water

Directions:
1. In a large pot, sauté onions in olive oil, cooking until soft, about 5 minutes.
2. Add garlic and carrots and cook until soft, a few minutes more.
3. Add Italian seasoning mix, bay leaf, salt, sugar, tomatoes, tomato sauce, and tomato paste and water. Bring to a boil, then reduce the heat to simmer for one or more hours. You can use the slow cooker for this.
4. Remove the bay leaf and puree if desired. Serve immediately, store the sauce in fridge for five days, or freeze it for later use.

Pizza Sauce

I used to buy pizza sauce at the store until I discovered how ridiculously simple it is to make it myself. I can whip this up in matter of minutes and usually freeze what I don't use for next time. It defrosts quickly, and I use it to make little pizzas for snacks and also for pizza night.

Serves: 4–6

Ingredients:
- 1 6-ounce can tomato paste
- ¾ cup water
- 1 Tbsp. olive oil

63

- 2 cloves garlic, minced
- ½ tsp. salt
- ½ tsp. sugar
- ¼ tsp. pepper
- 1 tsp. Italian seasoning mix

Directions:
1. In a medium bowl, mix all the ingredients together. If time permits, make earlier in the day or the night before so flavors can meld.

My other base sauces are included in the Main Dishes section.

Side Strategy

Over time, as kids accept more foods, the side strategy becomes less important. For example, my nine-year-old daughter will eat any pasta dish now, even lasagna. But my six-year-old son is another story. One thing he really enjoys is Trader Joe's turkey meatballs. I've chosen this as a side for Italian night because it's a quick protein source, and my son is always falling short on that food group. My daughter went through the carb stage, too, where she wanted mostly starchy foods like bread. But now she loves protein (except eggs, which my son will eat, go figure).

On Italian night, I always serve a salad. It just goes together, right? Pizza and salad. Lasagna and salad. Pasta and salad. On easy nights, like spaghetti and meatballs or slow-cooker vegetarian lasagna, I let my kids make their own salad. I have them choose between veggie and fruit options, and they can pick a dressing for dipping.

Truth be told, it can take children a while to warm up to salads. Charlotte reports that her 10-year-old will now eat plain romaine lettuce and has recently allowed avocado. "I'm hopeful we can continue to make the family salad more interesting," she says.

"For now, if I plan to put other ingredients in the salad, I make her a separate bowl."

One reader asked how to introduce lettuce to her toddler. I think small pieces of crispy romaine or even iceberg lettuce give kids the crunch factor they like and can be used for dipping in ranch or other dressings. Using lettuce instead of tortillas for taco night is another way to get children used to the texture of lettuce.

Salad Dressings

I rarely buy salad dressing anymore. Not only is it easy to make yourself, it also tastes better. Here are my favorite homemade dressings and salad combinations to help inspire you for your own repertoire. Just put all the ingredients in a small jar and shake. I like to make these ahead of time, so the flavors can meld. Double or triple the amounts (except for the garlic) if you're serving a big crowd.

Balsamic Dressing:
- ⅓ cup olive oil
- 2 Tbsp balsamic vinegar
- a splash of red wine vinegar
- a pinch of brown sugar
- 1 garlic clove, crushed

Italian Dressing:
- ⅓ cup olive oil
- 2 Tbsp. red wine vinegar
- a splash of lemon juice
- 1 garlic clove, crushed
- ½ tsp. Italian seasoning mix
- salt and pepper to taste

Mustardy Vinaigrette:
- ⅓ cup olive oil
- 2 Tbsp. red wine vinegar
- 1 tsp. Dijon mustard
- 1 tsp. honey
- 1 garlic clove, minced
- salt and pepper to taste

For cranberry vinaigrette, George recommends adding dried cranberries (microwave for 10 seconds with cranberry juice) into the mustardy vinaigrette, add a shallot, and skip the honey. The following Ranch recipe was adapted from Todd Wilbur's Top Secret Recipes.[9]

Ranch
- ⅓ cup mayonnaise
- ⅓ cup buttermilk
- ⅓ cup plain yogurt or sour cream
- ¼ tsp. parsley flakes
- ¼ tsp. onion powder
- ¼ tsp. garlic powder
- ⅛ tsp. pepper
- a pinch of thyme

For a thinner consistency, use ½ cup mayonnaise and ½ cup buttermilk.

Salads

I plan out my weekly salads to cut down on waste. Lately, I've been adding croutons to salads to entice my daughter, who picks out the croutons and just happens to eat some greens along with it. I also rotate Caesar salad, but I buy the kit at the store. Of course, I serve salads at other times, too, like on square-meal nights and with lunches.

For each of the recipes to follow, prepare all the ingredients and toss them together in a large bowl. Add dressing at the table, giving children the option to dip salad pieces in their dressing of choice. I purposely did not use exact-ingredients for these recipes because I think it's better to personalize your salads (plus, I never measure ingredients in salads).

Apple and Pecan
- spinach or spring mix
- diced red onion
- grated carrot
- dried cranberries
- pecans
- chopped apple
- feta cheese
- avocado (optional)
- balsamic dressing

Greens and Strawberries
- spinach or spring mix
- chopped strawberries
- toasted almonds
- feta cheese
- balsamic or Italian dressing

You can also substitute grapes and walnuts for the strawberries and almonds.

Greek Salad
- green leaf lettuce
- cherry tomatoes, cut in half (or another tomato variety)
- sliced red onion
- sliced green or red pepper

- peeled and chopped cucumbers
- olives (optional)
- feta cheese
- Italian dressing

Green Salad
- any green
- sliced red onion
- sliced yellow pepper
- sliced mushrooms
- carrots
- chopped tomatoes
- avocado
- croutons
- sunflower seeds
- feta or goat cheese
- any dressing

Spinach Salad
- spinach
- pear or apple slices
- sliced red onion
- dried cranberries
- candied pecans or walnuts
- sliced mushrooms
- feta or goat cheese
- mustardy or balsamic vinaigrette

Main Dishes

I like simple when it comes to Italian food. Next are the main dishes I include in my rotation.

Pasta Alfredo

I used to make a basic white sauce with milk, butter and flour, but it was mediocre at best. Then I tried all these different Alfredo recipes, but they were either too rich for weeknight meals or too time consuming. During my 30 Meal Challenge, I simplified the ingredients and found this to be the best combo for us. You may want yours to be more creamy and rich, but we like it light (*we* really means *me*, but hey, I'm the cook!). I use this amount of sauce for about a half pound of pasta—a meal for four. You can double it to make for a bigger crowd.

Serves: 4

Ingredients:
- ½ pound fettuccine
- 2 Tbsp. olive oil
- 2 garlic cloves, minced
- ¼ cup cream cheese
- ⅓ cup milk
- ⅓ cup Parmesan cheese, finely grated
- ½ cup chicken broth
- ½ tsp. salt
- ¼ tsp. white pepper
- ⅛ tsp. nutmeg
- parsley (optional)

Directions:
1. Cook fettuccine according to package directions, drain and set aside.
2. In a large saucepan over medium heat, add oil and garlic and cook until fragment, about 1 minute. Add the rest of the

ingredients and mix until well combined and heated through. Turn off heat and set aside.

3. Add the fettuccine and any additional ingredients like chopped chicken, cooked shrimp and steamed or roasted vegetables to the sauce. Mix until well combined and serve immediately.

Shrimp Linguine

This recipe is adapted from Weekly Bite's Simple Shrimp Scampi with Linguine recipe.[10] Estela, dietitian and creator of the site, has amazing recipes that are healthy, too. While this recipe calls for shrimp, it can definitely be made vegetarian by adding roasted or steamed vegetables, or it can be used with ravioli topped with nuts. I also found a great whole-grain linguine pasta (Barilla brand) that works well here. I love this dish's simple ingredients: garlic, olive oil, lemon and salt.

George tried this and loved the result. "It's a simple meal and easy to throw together," he says. "Frozen shrimp can be thawed (under cold running water) in the time it takes the water to boil for the pasta. Just pair with grilled asparagus or another veggie to round out the meal."

Serves: 4

Ingredients:

- ½ pound whole-grain linguine
- 1 pound frozen raw shrimp
- 1 Tbsp. butter
- 2 Tbsp. olive oil
- 2–3 garlic cloves, minced
- ½ lemon, juiced
- ½ tsp. salt
- ¼ tsp. pepper
- ¼ tsp. red pepper flakes (optional)

- parsley
- 2 heaping Tbsp. grated Parmesan cheese (optional)

Directions:

1. Cook pasta according to the package directions. Defrost the shrimp in cold water. While the pasta is cooking, put the olive oil, butter and garlic in a large saucepan and cook until garlic becomes fragrant, about 1 minute.
2. Add lemon juice, salt, pepper and shrimp to the saucepan. Cook the shrimp about 5 minutes or until cooked through (they will be pink). Add in pasta, red pepper and Parmesan and mix until well combined. Top with parsley.

Meat Lasagna

Everyone needs a couple of lasagna recipes, even if they're just for making for someone in need. I rotate this with slow-cooker veggie lasagna.[11] This meal came together relatively easy. The best thing about lasagna is that you can make it the night before or earlier in the day and just pop it in the oven later. And the leftovers taste even better.

Serves: 6–8

Ingredients:

- 1 Tbsp. olive oil
- 1 pound lean ground meat of choice
- 2 garlic cloves, minced
- ½ medium onion, diced
- 1 small red, yellow or green bell pepper (optional)
- 3 cups homemade or jarred marinara sauce
- 8 oz. shredded mozzarella cheese, divided
- 1 cup shredded carrots
- 1 egg

- 15 oz. ricotta (made with skim or whole milk)
- ¼ tsp. garlic powder
- ¼ cup Parmesan cheese, divided
- 9 dried lasagna noodles

Directions:

1. Cook noodles according to package directions, cool and set aside. Preheat the oven to 350°F.

2. In a large pot over medium-high heat, add the onion and oil and sauté until softened, about 5 minutes. Add garlic for the last minute of cooking time. Add the meat and cook through. Drain off any fat and add the marinara sauce. Bring to a boil, then reduce the heat to low.

3. Put the shredded carrots in a microwave-safe medium bowl and cook for 2 minutes. Add half of the mozzarella, the egg, ricotta cheese and garlic powder. Stir until well combined.

4. Spray a 9x13-inch casserole dish with cooking spray and spread 1 cup of the meat sauce on the bottom. Place three noodles on top of the meat sauce, then spread 1 cup of the cheese mixture, ¾ cup of the meat and half of the Parmesan over the noodles. Repeat one more time and finish with cheese, meat sauce and the rest of the mozzarella cheese.

5. Bake, covered, for 40 minutes. Remove foil and bake for an additional 5 minutes.

Pasta Primavera

My love for summer veggies and the need for a Tried and True pasta primavera recipe led to this combo. I season it with my Italian seasoning mix. Got it on the first try!

Serves: 4

Ingredients:

- ½ pound bowtie pasta
- 4 Tbsp. olive oil, divided
- 2 carrots, sliced
- 2 zucchinis, cut into matchsticks
- 1 red or yellow bell pepper, sliced
- ½ red onion, sliced
- 1½ tsp. Italian seasoning mix
- ¼ tsp. salt
- 3 garlic cloves, minced
- ½ cup chicken or vegetable broth
- salt and pepper to taste
- ⅓ cup Parmesan cheese

Directions:

1. Cook pasta according to package directions and set aside.
2. Preheat oven to 400°F. Combine vegetables with 2 Tbsp. oil, Italian mix and salt. Place on a large baking sheet and cook for 25 minutes.
3. Heat 2 Tbsp. oil in a large pot over medium-high heat. Add garlic. Once the garlic sizzles, add broth, veggies, pasta and parmesan cheese. Season with salt and pepper.

Pizza night

Since I started cooking, I have been on a mission to make a homemade thin pizza crust. I almost gave up until I found a specific strategy detailed on PizzaMaking.com.[12] The key is to use flour with at least 12 percent gluten or higher (I use King Arthur bread flour) and refrigerate the dough for 24 hours. I don't have a standing mixer, so I use my bread machine to knead the dough. I just stick to the recipe provided with my bread machine but use high-gluten flour. Katja likes the King Arthur cookbook pizza dough recipe for her family's weekly homemade pizza night. The day before pizza night, I make the dough and refrigerate it for about 24 hours. I take it out an hour or two before dinnertime. I preheat the oven to 450°F and spray the back of two baking pans with cooking spray. Then, I massage the dough out on the back of the pans, getting it as thin as I can, making two pies. I put the dough in the oven for about 5 minutes, just enough for the bottom to get a little crispy.

Once the dough is precooked, I add the toppings and transfer to a pizza stone for an additional 7–8 minutes of cooking at the same temperature. Be sure the pizza stone has been in the oven this whole time, getting nice and hot. This results in a beautiful, crispy crust.

George has decided he doesn't want to bother with homemade pizza dough. "Skip the fuss of homemade crust and let the pros handle it," he says. "We found an excellent *real* dough in our grocery store's freezer section. We just have to take it out of the freezer the night before and let it warm to room temperature for about an hour or two before using it."

Spaghetti and Meatballs or Ground Meat

This is the easiest meal I have, and it's one the whole family likes. I use my homemade marinara, but I also always have jarred pasta sauce on hand just in case. I alternate between cooking ground meat (see recipe below) and heating up Trader Joe's turkey meatballs. I use whole-grain spaghetti and make a salad.

Serves: 4-6

Ingredients:
- 1 Tbsp. olive oil
- ½ cup finely chopped onion
- 1-2 garlic cloves
- 1 pound lean ground meat of choice

- 1 jar marinara sauce (store bought or homemade)

Directions:

1. In a medium sauce pan, cook onions in oil over medium-high heat until fragrant. Add meat and stir until cooked through. Add garlic the last minute or two of cooking.

2. When the meat is cooked through, drain the excess fat and add the marinara sauce. Once the mixture boils, turn down heat and simmer until pasta is done and the meal is ready to be served.

Cooking Jobs for Kids

Young, beginner cooks (five years old and under) can:
- Measure ingredients
- Assist boiling pasta
- Stir sauces
- Tear lettuce
- Wash veggies

Older, more experienced cooks (six years old and over) can:
- Cook pasta
- Pull together simple salads
- Make marinades
- Chop veggies (assist as needed)
- Follow a simple recipe

Goals

I would like to eventually incorporate a pesto pasta dish and try different raviolis and stuffed shell meals. I will also continue to change up what goes into my Alfredo and other base sauces. And maybe, eventually, I'll bring in some Italian desserts like Cannoli. Now it's time to branch out even more.

8 ASIAN AND GREEK INSPIRED MEALS

When it came to cultural cuisine, I felt ready to move beyond my comfort zone of Mexican and Italian. I wanted a few Asian-inspired meals, but I wasn't ready to take on sushi. I could handle a versatile Chinese stir-fry and easy fried rice recipe. I love Greek food, so I wanted a good chicken and falafel dish, and both my husband and I have always enjoyed curry. These meals seemed like good places to start. In the future—and especially after mastering these—I'd love to beef up my ethnic dishes.

Main Dishes

Here's what I have in my rotation for Asian and Greek inspired meals.

Stir-Fry Base Sauce

I always hear that Chinese stir-fry is easy to make, but I've struggled with it mainly due to the sauce. My stir-fries have always been passable, but when I pushed for ratings, my husband would always say, "It's missing MSG or something." I've tried a variety of sauces that just kind of fell flat. Without a regular sauce recipe to get excited about, Chinese stir-fry was an infrequent guest at our dinner table.

After refocusing my efforts and trying another half dozen recipes, I finally came up with a sauce that wows us! This was inspired by Recipe Tin Eats' All-Purpose Stir Fry Sauce.[13] I make this sauce to serve our family of four, which covers about 1 pound of chicken or shrimp and 3-4 cups of veggies. My side strategy is to serve the stir-fry with fruit and store-bought egg rolls. I alternate between making Chinese noodles and rice.

Ingredients:

- 2 Tbsp. reduced sodium soy sauce
- 2 Tbsp. oyster sauce
- ½ Tbsp. brown sugar
- 1 tsp. pure sesame oil
- ½ tsp. Shaoxing (rice wine) or substitute with dry sherry
- ½ tsp. white pepper
- 1 garlic clove, minced

What's nice about stir-fry is that anything goes. For a protein source, we gravitate towards chicken. My favorite veggies to stir fry are broccoli, red peppers, onions, carrots and snow peas. I usually steam denser veggies like broccoli first. These are the key steps to ensure stir-fries turn out well:

1. When possible, make the sauce ahead and add the garlic so the flavors can meld. Also, marinade the protein with 1 Tbsp. soy sauce and 1 Tbsp. dry sherry for an hour or more.

2. Wait for the skillet or wok to become hot before adding food.

3. Stir fry in batches. Adding too much food in the wok or skillet at one time can make food soggy.

4. Cook the protein in oil first and set it aside in a bowl when it's done.

5. After the protein is done, stir fry veggies that take longer to cook first (carrots, broccoli), followed by quick-cooking veggies (mushrooms, zucchini, bell peppers). Super-fast-cooking veggies, like greens, should always be put in last.

6. Add garlic and ginger (1 Tbsp. each) towards the end of cooking to keep them from burning and to help flavor the whole dish. For example, add garlic and ginger when starting on the veggies after the protein is cooked.

7. When veggies are done combine the protein, veggies and sauce. Add about 2 teaspoons of corn starch to thicken the sauce. Serve over rice or noodles.

Teriyaki Slow-Cooker Chicken

Finding a Tried and True teriyaki chicken recipe proved to be quite difficult. To be honest, I kind of gave up until I spotted Crockpot Chicken Teriyaki on the Wannabite blog.[14] Yes, it calls for teriyaki sauce, but adding the soy sauce, garlic and brown sugar makes this sauce especially worthy. It's great in the slow cooker, or it can be used as a sauce for stir-fry or grilling.

    Charlotte tried this with her family, and it was a real hit! She used boneless chicken breasts and said the meat turned out a bit on the dry side. I never have that problem when using chicken thighs.

Serves: 4–6

Ingredients:
- 1 pound boneless, skinless chicken thighs
- ⅓ cup teriyaki sauce or marinade
- 2 Tbsp. reduced sodium soy sauce
- 1 tsp. grated or ¼ tsp. dried ginger
- 3 garlic cloves, minced

- ¼ cup brown sugar
- ½ cup chicken broth
- ½ tsp. onion powder
- 1 tsp. cornstarch
- sesame seeds (optional)

Directions:
1. Place chicken in a slow cooker. Mix the next seven ingredients in a medium bowl then transfer to the slow cooker, covering the chicken. Cook on high for 4 hours or on low for 6 hours. Before it's done, steam your veggies of choice.
2. When the chicken and vegetables are cooked, transfer the sauce to a pan and heat over medium heat. Add the cornstarch, stirring to thicken. Cut the chicken into bite-size pieces (this can be done earlier—it's up to you).
3. Combine the sauce, chicken and veggies. Top with sesame seeds and serve.

Fried Rice

Everyone needs a good fried-rice recipe, right? I looked and looked until I discovered "5 Secrets to Making Fabulous Fried Rice" on Patricia Tanumihardja's site, The Asian Grandmothers Cookbook.[15] Her site, and book of the same name, provides recipes and tips to get Asian cooking right.

Fried rice is a great avenue for using up leftovers, whether it's chicken, pork or cooking up something quick like shrimp or tofu. It works nicely as a side dish, too.

Serves: 4

Ingredients:
- 4 cups cooked long- or medium-grain rice (day-old rice is preferred, I use brown rice)
- 1 tablespoon neutral oil like canola
- 2 cloves garlic, minced
- ½ cup yellow onion, coarsely chopped

- 1 cup carrots, chopped small
- 3 eggs
- 1 cup chopped leftover meat or tofu
- ½ cup frozen peas, defrosted
- 2 Tbsp. oyster sauce
- 2 Tbsp. reduced sodium soy sauce
- salt
- white pepper

Directions:
1. Heat a wok or skillet on high heat for about 1 minute, then add oil. Once the oil gets hot, reduce heat to medium and add the garlic and onion and stir until fragrant, about 30 seconds. Add the carrots, stirring until tender, about 2–3 minutes.
2. Move all the ingredients to one side of the skillet or wok. Add the eggs and scramble until cooked but still moist. Add the protein, peas and rice, stirring as each item is added.
3. Add the soy and oyster sauces, then add the salt and white pepper to taste. Stir everything until it is well combined and heated through, about 3–4 minutes. If the rice begins to stick to the pan, add more oil.

Greek Chicken Pitas

Greek chicken, pita bread, hummus, tzatziki… I love it all. A while back, I searched for chicken pita recipes, and the meal below has just kind of evolved from those early efforts. Now, this meal is one of my favorite Tried and True family dinners, and I also make it for Saturday lunches. I choose this meal for those nights we need to rush to eat before an event. I put out chicken, hummus, tzatziki, pita bread, tomatoes, red onion and feta on the counter for quick meal assembly. Because it's a sandwich, no utensils are required (read: fewer dishes).

"I made the Greek pitas last night with Mediterranean chicken I had from Costco," says Cari. "Everyone liked it, which is a miracle!"

Serves: 4

Ingredients:
- 1–1½ pound boneless, skinless chicken thighs
- ½ tsp. salt
- ½ tsp. garlic powder
- ½ tsp. thyme
- ½ tsp. oregano
- ⅛ tsp. pepper
- ½ cup chicken broth
- 1 Tbsp. olive oil
- ¼ cup plain yogurt
- 1 Tbsp. balsamic vinegar
- ½ red onion, sliced
- 2 medium tomatoes cut in wedges or chopped
- ⅓ cup feta cheese
- 6–8 whole-wheat pita bread halves

Vinegar Mix
- 2 Tbsp. olive oil
- 1 Tbsp. red wine vinegar
- ½ tsp. dried oregano
- salt and pepper, to taste

Tzatziki Sauce
- ½ cup plain yogurt
- 1 garlic clove, minced
- ¼ cup peeled and diced cucumber
- ½ lemon, juiced
- ¼ tsp. dried dill
- ¼ tsp. salt

Directions:

1. In a medium bowl, add the spices, broth, balsamic vinegar, yogurt and stir to combine. Place the chicken in a slow cooker and top with broth mixture. Turn the slow cooker on low for 5–7 hours or on high for 3–5. Cooking times will vary based on the slow cooker.

2. Mix together the tzatziki ingredients and put in the fridge at least an hour before serving, so the flavors can meld.

3. When the chicken is done and you are ready to get dinner ready, preheat the oven to 200°F. Wrap the pitas in foil and put them in the oven.

4. Make the vinegar mix by whisking together the olive oil, vinegar, oregano, salt and pepper. Prepare the tomatoes and onions and place in a medium bowl, and then mix in the feta cheese. Pour the vinegar mix over the veggies and stir until well combined.

5. Remove chicken and put on a cutting board, cut it into chunks and then place it in serving bowl topping with leftover juices.

6. Take pitas out of the oven and place on a plate. Serve chicken and pitas with veggie mix, tzatziki and hummus (optional). Have everyone make his or her own pita.

Falafel Pitas

I also wanted a vegetarian dish to substitute for chicken and got stuck on the idea of baked falafel. Each time I made it, something just wasn't right. Sometimes the flavor was okay, but it would be too hard or too soft. Then I'd get the texture down, but the flavor seemed off. In the end, I found dried chickpeas turn out better than canned. It takes some planning to remember to soak the beans at night, but it's worth it.

Ingredients:

- 1½ cups dried chickpeas (or 2 15-oz, rinsed and drained), reserving some liquid from soaking
- ½ onion, chopped

- 3–4 garlic cloves, chopped
- ½ cup cilantro
- ½ Tbsp. cumin
- 1 tsp. coriander
- ¼ tsp. red pepper flakes (more if you like it hotter)
- 1 tsp. salt
- ¼ tsp. pepper
- ½ tsp. baking soda
- ½ lemon, juiced
- ¼ cup olive oil

Directions:
1. Soak chickpeas in water overnight. Drain and rinse the next day, saving at least ¼ cup water. If you are using canned beans, you will not need the added water.
2. Preheat oven to 375°F. Place all the ingredients except the chickpea water in a food processor and pulse until well combined but not pureed. Feel the mixture with your hand. If it's too dry, add water, a little bit at a time.
3. Once the texture is mealy enough, meaning it easily forms into a ball using your hands, place about 15 balls on a baking sheet sprayed with cooking spray. Brush each ball with olive oil.
4. Bake for 10 minutes, remove from the oven and flip each ball, brushing olive oil on the other side, and return to the oven. After another 10 minutes, turn oven to broil for a few minutes and remove once browned (check frequently!). Serve with same items listed in the Greek Chicken Pita recipe.

Red Curry Sauce

I wasn't satisfied with a curry recipe until I tried Pinch of Yum's Red Thai Curry Sauce.[16] You can skip the crushed peanuts or serve them on the side. Use as a sauce for cooked lentils, chickpeas, chicken or any cooked vegetables. This is new in the rotation, so

I'm hoping my kids will learn to like it over time. My side strategy is to serve it alongside fruit and Naan bread. When it comes to new sauces, I encourage my kids to watch me make it so they can see what goes into it. Then at dinner, they can use a napkin to wipe up part of the sauce, if they want less of it or sometimes I put the sauce on the side so they can dip.

Finding versatile sauces for ethnic dishes is key. Charlotte regularly makes an Indian vegetarian curry with chickpeas and added veggies over brown rice, and Carey makes noodles with peanut sauce.

Cooking Jobs for Kids

Young, beginner cooks (five years old and under) can:
- Help measure ingredients for sauces
- Assist stirring the stir-fry
- Wash vegetables
- Put food in the food processor and turn it on

Older, more experienced cooks (six years old and over) can:
- Prepare the chicken for chicken pitas
- Make stir-fry sauce
- Chop veggies (with assistance as needed)
- Soak and sort the beans

Goals

I would really like to expand upon my ethnic meals, but for now, mastering and improving on these dishes is my main goal. When I'm ready to move forward, my first new meal will be pad Thai.

Let's move on to square meals.

9 SQUARE MEALS AND SIDES

Having too many meal components used to stress me out. I call these types of dishes "square meals" because they typically contain a protein, a starch, a veggie and fruit. I've made many mistakes while making these meals, including choosing the wrong sides and not timing everything right, but I have learned how to pull it all together so it's not so stressful.

Mastering a core set of side dishes to mix and match with main dishes has helped me a lot. For example, if I'm using the oven to cook fish, I won't roast veggies unless I do it earlier in the day. It might be better to have a salad or stir-fry some veggies. The more I plan the right sides, the better square meals turn out.

Here's a list of square meals and sides I include in my rotation. First are the protein sources, followed by starchy sides and ending with veggies. For grilled main meals and sides see the next chapter and don't forget the salads from Chapter 7.

Protein Sources

I always build my square meals around a protein source. Next are the ones included in my rotation.

Salmon Prepared Three Ways

I have tried numerous preparation methods for salmon, my all-time favorite fish. I used to put it in foil and cook for about 40 minutes, which helps it stay moist. I've tried it in the slow cooker, which I don't recommend. I've attempted mustardy-type seasonings and the sweeter varieties. Now, I opt for easy baking (or grilling in the summer) and season it one of three ways. I make trout the same way, which is equally as tasty.

1. Easy Rub

I got this rub recipe from my friend, Holly, who is an awesome cook. I keep it in a container ready to go. I apply a small amount of olive oil to the fish to moisten it and rub in the rub, which is equal parts of each ingredient.

Ingredients:
- 1 Tbsp. cumin
- 1 Tbsp. curry powder
- 1 Tbsp. coriander
- 1 Tbsp. chili powder
- 1 Tbsp. sugar
- 1 Tbsp. salt

Directions:
1. Combine all the spices together. Transfer to a container for storage.

2. Dried Basil and Garlic

This was inspired by All Recipe's Baked Salmon recipe I stumbled upon years ago.[17] Sometimes I also top the salmon with mushrooms, spinach and tomatoes before baking.

Serves: 4

Ingredients:
- 1 pound salmon fillet
- 2 Tbsp. olive oil
- 1 Tbsp. lemon juice
- 2 garlic cloves minced
- 1 tsp. dried basil
- ½ tsp. salt
- ¼ tsp. pepper

Directions:
1. Preheat oven to 400F. In a small bowl, combine all of the ingredients and pour on top of salmon with a spoon.
2. Bake salmon in the oven for 13-17 minutes depending on the fish's thickness.

3. Fish Nuggets

Nuggets made with salmon are what got my daughter loving fish, which is one her favorite meals to this day. I no longer make them nugget style, but I do top some of the salmon with breading mix at her request. I basically mix breadcrumbs with Parmesan cheese, garlic powder and salt.

Charlotte shares her secret weapon for enticing kids to eat fish. "Serve fish with rice, veggies, and small seaweed papers," she says. "Then, let the kids make their own mini hand rolls at the table. You could call them Japanese tacos, too."

Serves: 4

Ingredients:
- 1 pound salmon fillet
- 1 quarter stick of butter, melted
- ½ cup bread crumbs

- ½ cup parmesan cheese
- ½ tsp. garlic powder
- ½ tsp. salt

Directions:
1. Preheat oven to 400 F. Cut fish into 1 - 1.5 inch pieces.
2. In a small bowl mix the bread crumbs parmesan cheese, garlic powder and salt. In another small bowl melt the butter by microwaving it for a few seconds.
3. Dip each piece of salmon into the melted butter, roll in bread crumb mix and place on a baking sheet lined with foil. Bake for 8-10 minutes or cooked all the way through. Serve immediately.

George points out that quality salmon doesn't need to be sauced up. "Try grilling it or broiling with just a little olive oil, sea salt, and pepper," he says. Charlotte likes to add teriyaki sauce to her salmon, which is something you can buy or make yourself with soy sauce, brown sugar and garlic.

Chicken Tenders

I cook with chicken a lot, so I haven't spent too much time coming up with a square meal. Meghan uses her mother-in-law's roast chicken recipe, which calls for softened butter mixed with parsley, thyme, rosemary, minced garlic and ½ chili chopped finely. "Loosen the skin around the neck and slather about half to three quarters of the butter mixture under the skin," she says. "Then dab the rest on the thighs and outside of skin. Roast till juices run clear."

When I choose chicken for square-meal night, I either slow-cook drumsticks with a bunch of garlic or make chicken tenders. Believe it or not, my husband and I have come to like this chicken tender meal more than our kids.

Serves: 4

Ingredients:
- 1 egg, beaten or 1 quarter stick of butter, melted
- 1 pound boneless, skinless chicken tenders or breasts, cut into 1–2-inch pieces
- ¾ cup bread crumbs
- ⅓ cup Parmesan cheese, finely grated
- ½ tsp. paprika
- ½ tsp. garlic powder
- ½ tsp. mustard seed
- ½ tsp. salt
- ¼ tsp. pepper

Honey Mustard Sauce
- 3 Tbsp. Dijon mustard
- 3 Tbsp. honey
- 3 Tbsp. plain low-fat yogurt

Directions:
1. Preheat oven to 400°F. Crack an egg (or use butter for a richer nugget) and beat in a small bowl. Cut the chicken tender pieces in half. Combine dry ingredients and spices in a medium bowl.
2. Dip chicken in egg or butter and then dredge well through the dry-spice mixture, using your hands to add more mixture on top so they are thoroughly coated.
3. Place chicken on a cookie sheet lined with foil and sprayed with cooking spray or parchment paper. Cook for 20–22 minutes or until chicken is cooked through.
4. Serve with a honey mustard sauce by mixing Dijon mustard, honey and plain yogurt (or mayo) in a small bowl.

Pork Tenderloin

With a slow-cooker that runs a bit high temperature-wise, lean pork tenderloin slow cooked always turns out too dry. I spotted Ellie Kreiger's Pork Tenderloin with Seasoned Rub recipe on the Food

Network that called for baking.[18] The first time I made it, without any changes, it turned out *perfecto.*

Fish Cakes

This meal wins the prize for "most attempts." The thing is, I think I have a favorite recipe, but when I make it the second or third time, I find fault with it. I started out using canned salmon but have switched over to canned tuna or mackerel. The canned salmon is just too fishy for me. I tried it with sweet potatoes, stuffing mix (actually not bad, but have you seen the ingredients in stuffing mixes?) and a variety of spices. Simple wins out again: garlic, lemon, Dijon mustard and salt. Although it's not my preferred cooking method, pan-frying is the only way to go to get crispy cakes.

Meghan likes to use potatoes rather than breadcrumbs, boiling until soft and mashing. Jen, who tried the recipe, liked using tuna instead of salmon. "The recipe was a hit with me and my husband (no taste from my three-year-old, even though he has eaten fish in the past)," she says. "We served it with ketchup and talked about trying it with Old Bay seasoning next time to give it a bit of a crab-cake flavor."

Coming up with the right sauce has been tough because I'm not really a fan of tartar or remoulade sauces, which are often paired with fish cakes. For us, a good ranch dressing does the trick (pg. 66).

Serves: 4-6

Ingredients:
- 2 small cans of tuna (10-12 oz. total)
- 1 Tbsp. plain yogurt
- 1 tsp. Dijon mustard
- ½ lemon, juiced

- ½ tsp. lemon zest
- 2 garlic cloves, minced
- ¼ cup green onions, chopped
- ½ tsp. salt
- ¼ tsp. pepper
- 1 cup breadcrumbs
- 2 eggs

Directions:

1. In a medium bowl, mix together the first nine ingredients with a spoon until well combined. Add the breadcrumbs and eggs and combine (I like using my hands at this point).
2. Form into about 7–8 patties. If time allows, store in the fridge for about 30 minutes to help keep the patties together.
3. Coat a fry pan with canola oil and turn the stove on to medium-high heat. Once hot, add the fish cakes. Cook for 3–5 minutes per side, turning down the heat as needed.

Baked Lentils & Brown Rice

Food.com's Brown Rice and Lentil Casserole isn't your typical square meal because it's actually a casserole that can be made into a one-pot dish.[19] I tried this recipe years ago, and I couldn't get over how easy and tasty it was. You can add any spices and veggies you want and serve it with fruit, salad or any veggie. Carey liked this meal so much, she made it into a freezer meal to have again in a couple of weeks.

Baked Shrimp

I've really come to enjoy cooking with shrimp. It defrosts in cold water in minutes and cooks very quickly, making it a good protein option for meals. Charlotte uses a very easy marinade for shrimp, which is just mayo plus Herbes de Provence. She says the exact measurements don't really matter: "Just make sure there is enough mayo to cover the shrimp and generously season it with Herbes de Provence." She either grills or pan-fries the shrimp.

I have found that baking shrimp is one of the easiest ways to make it. I've tried it a few different ways, but this breadcrumb and Parmesan mixture is what I've been doing lately. This is easy to change up based on your tastes.

Serves: 4

Ingredients:

- 1 pound frozen raw, deveined shrimp
- 3 Tbsp. olive oil
- 1 Tbsp. lemon juice
- 3 garlic cloves, minced
- ¼ cup bread crumbs
- ¼ cup finely grated Parmesan cheese
- ¼ tsp. salt
- ¼ tsp. paprika
- ¼ tsp. mustard powder
- salt and pepper, to taste
- parsley (for garnish)

Directions:

1. Preheat the oven to 400°F. In a small bowl combine the olive oil, lemon juice and garlic. Pour this mixture until it covers an entire 9x13 glass dish. Place shrimp in the dish and toss them until lightly coated with the oil mixture.
2. In a small bowl or cup, place the Parmesan cheese, breadcrumbs and spices. Sprinkle the breadcrumb mixture, some parsley and a bit of salt and pepper over each shrimp.
3. Bake for 10 minutes. Serve immediately over pasta, rice or quinoa.

Starchy Sides

If the protein doesn't have starch in it, I always serve the meal with one, whether it's potatoes or whole grains. Here are my main starchy sides.

Mashed Potatoes

There are many different ways to make mashed potatoes. Katja prefers the classic way: butter, milk, salt and pepper. Charlotte admits, "I love eating mashed potatoes, but I hate making them! My daughter believes you can only have them on Thanksgiving (when Grandma cooks them)."

I was attracted to this Olive Oil Mashed Potatoes with Garlic recipe on Cook for Your Life blog because it uses olive oil and garlic instead of cream or butter.[20] This is simple and has a nice flavor. I usually make more and freeze the extra for quick future meals.

Serves: 4–6

Ingredients:
- 1½ pound Yukon Gold potatoes, peeled and cubed
- ⅓ cup olive oil
- 3 whole garlic cloves
- 1 Tbsp. salt
- black pepper, to taste
- chopped flat-leaf parsley (optional)

Directions:
1. Place potatoes in a medium pot covered with about 1 inch of water and add salt. Bring to a boil and then turn down the heat. Cover and cook for about 15 minutes or until tender.
2. While potatoes are cooking, pour olive oil in a small sauce pan

and turn heat to low. Add intact garlic cloves, cooking on low for about 20 minutes. Remove the garlic-oil mixture from heat when the garlic turns a deep gold and dispose of the garlic.
3. Drain the potatoes, saving some of the potato water in a cup, and return them to the same pot. Stir in the garlic-infused olive oil and enough potato water until they reach your desired consistency. Mix in parsley and serve.

Oven-Roasted Potatoes

I think everyone needs a Tried and True recipe for roasted potatoes. From what I've read, red or Yukon Gold potatoes are the best potatoes for roasting. I usually buy about 1½ pounds of either potatoes and cut them into even pieces: the smaller and the more uniform, the better.

Jen lets us in on her secret: "Because we live near the Chesapeake Bay, Old Bay seasoning is in our blood, and we put it on everything. Red potatoes are no exception. When we roast them, we coat the chopped potatoes in olive oil and then sprinkle (generously) with Old Bay, or a homemade Old Bay mix. Doesn't get any easier than that!"

Serves: 4-6

Ingredients:

- 1½–2 pounds red or Yukon Gold potatoes
- 2 Tbsp. olive oil
- 2–4 garlic cloves, minced
- 1–2 Tbsp. rosemary (for red) or thyme (for gold), or about 1 tsp. if using dried herbs
- ½ tsp. salt
- pepper, to taste

Directions:

1. Cut the potatoes into wedges and drop in ice-cold water for 30 minutes (this is to draw out the starch). Preheat oven to 450°F.
2. Dry the potatoes with a paper towel and place them in a big bowl. Add oil, garlic, spice, salt and pepper and mix using your hands. Lay the potato wedges flat on large metal pan and roast for about 30 minutes or until browned (check them after 20 minutes).

Roasted Sweet Potatoes

I never ate sweet potatoes until I was a mom. When I introduced my daughter to solids, I tried them out. Not only did she love them, but so did I. Ellie Kreiger's Honey Roasted Sweet Potatoes on the Food Network is my favorite go-to recipe for sweet potatoes.[21] Simply add honey, olive oil, lemon juice and some salt.

Baked Brown Rice

Oven-baked brown is fail-proof! Alton Brown's Baked Brown Rice recipe on the Food Network is an easy one to change up.[22] Add different spices and veggies or keep it simple. Make it on a lazy Sunday afternoon and freeze for quick weekday meals.

Quinoa with Sautéed Veggies

I'm a late adopter when it comes to trying trendy foods. When I heard of quinoa, I took my sweet time incorporating it into my menu. I read that it works well in the rice cooker, so that's what I went with, and it turned out perfectly. It is especially good with veggies sautéed in olive oil. This can go for any grain; sauté onions, garlic and some veggies and cook it in broth, and you've got a versatile side.

Serves: 4–6

Ingredients:
- 1 cup quinoa (rinsed in a fine-mesh colander, if you have one)
- 2 cups chicken or vegetable broth
- 2 Tbsp. olive oil
- ½ cup chopped onion
- 1 cup chopped carrots
- 2–3 garlic cloves, minced
- 3–4 handfuls of baby spinach (or other green), chopped
- salt and pepper, to taste
- Parmesan cheese (optional)

Directions:
1. Put broth and quinoa in rice cooker and turn on.
2. While quinoa is cooking, sauté onion and carrots in oil in a small sauce pan until softened, about 5 minutes. Add the garlic and spinach and sauté another minute.
3. Turn heat to low and cover until carrots soften, about 5–10 minutes. When quinoa is done, let it sit for 5–10 minutes, then add to the veggies and stir. Add salt and pepper to taste and Parmesan cheese, if desired. Serve warm.

Veggies

It's important to have a decent variety of veggies to serve and expose kids to. I'm a huge fan of roasting, but I also try to branch out with other cooking methods. Of course, there are always salads (see Chapter 7).

Roasted Veggies

I used to prefer salads to cooked veggies until I discovered roasting. After doing some research about the dos and don'ts, I found the following roasting tips:

1. Use a large metal pan with short sides (Instead of a casserole dish). This allows the moisture to escape, so veggies are crispy, not soggy.

2. Cut veggies in uniform pieces. Thick veggies like root vegetables and squash can be cut into 1–2-inch pieces, but flowery veggies like broccoli and cauliflower can be a bit bigger.

3. Use the right amount of oil: just enough so each piece looks shiny but not drenched and greasy.

4. Choose the right oil. Different oils have different smoke points (the temperature at which oil smokes and starts to breakdown). A high-quality extra virgin olive oil has a smoke point between 365–400°F, according to the Olive Oil Source.[23] Although it is unlikely that roasting at high temperatures (450°F as recommended below) means the oil reaches that temperature, to play it safe, choose an oil with a higher smoke point like avocado oil or a more refined olive oil (called light or extra light olive oil). At lower temperatures, a quality extra virgin olive oil is fine.

5. Give veggies room to breathe. Too much crowding doesn't let steam escape (read: you'll get soggy veggies).

6. Go for high heat. Most cooking websites recommend at least 450°F, so the outside gets crispy and the inside stays soft. But I think it really depends on personal preference. Play around with temps and what works best for you. I never go below 400°F, though.

While you can roast any veggie, here are my favorites I rotate on a regular basis.

Asparagus

Serves: 4-6

Ingredients:

- 1 pound green (or white) asparagus stalks, ends cut off
- 1–2 Tbsp. extra virgin olive oil
- ⅓ cup grated Parmesan cheese
- salt and pepper, to taste

Directions:
1. Preheat oven to 425°F. Arrange asparagus on baking sheet. Toss asparagus stalks with olive oil and sprinkle salt, pepper and Parmesan over stalks evenly. Roast for about 15 minutes or until stalks are tender.

Broccoli

This was inspired by "The Best Broccoli of Your Life" on the Amateur Gourmet blog.[24] It doesn't getter better than roasting broccoli.

Serves: 4

Ingredients:

- 1 12-oz package raw broccoli or large head of broccoli, separated into florets
- 2½ Tbsp. oil, divided
- 2 garlic cloves, minced
- ¼ tsp. salt and pepper
- 2 Tbsp. Parmesan cheese

- ½ lemon, juiced

Directions:
1. Heat the oven to 425°F. Toss the broccoli with 2 Tbsp. oil, garlic, salt and pepper. Roast on a baking sheet for 20–25 minutes. 2. Remove from the oven and place in a bowl. Add Parmesan cheese, lemon and remaining ½ Tbsp. oil.

Cauliflower

If you don't think you like cauliflower, you just haven't had it roasted yet! I originally spotted Roasted Cauliflower on All Recipes and have adapted it to our tastes.[25]

Serves: 4

Ingredients:
- 1 large head cauliflower, separated into florets (or 12 ounce package raw cauliflower)
- 3-4 garlic cloves, minced
- 2 Tbsp. light olive oil or avocado oil
- ¼ cup grated Parmesan cheese
- salt and black pepper to taste
- 1 tablespoon chopped fresh parsley (optional)

Directions:
1. Preheat the oven to 450°F and coat a large metal pan with cooking spray. Mix the cauliflower, oil and garlic in a large bowl or zipper-lock bag.
2. Spread the cauliflower on the pan, sprinkling with salt and pepper. Bake for about 15 minute and gently stir cauliflower and cook for an addition 10 minutes.
3. Take cauliflower out of the oven and sprinkle with Parmesan cheese and parsley, then broil for a few more minutes or until golden brown.

Summer Veggies

Roasted summer veggies is perfect tossed with pasta.

Serves: 4-6

Ingredients:
- 2–3 carrots, sliced
- 2 yellow squash, sliced
- 2 medium zucchini, sliced
- 1 red pepper, cut into strips
- ½ red onion, thinly sliced
- 2-3 Tbsp light olive oil or avocado oil
- 2 tsp. Italian seasoning mix (pg. 61)
- salt and pepper, to taste
- Parmesan cheese (optional)

Directions:
1. Preheat oven to 450°F. Cut all veggies in similar sizes and put in a large bowl. Add olive oil, salt and seasonings and mix until well combined.
2. Place on large metal pan and roast for about 20 minutes, stirring halfway through.

Sautéed Veggies

Having a handful of sauté recipes comes in handy for quick meals. George likes spinach and mushrooms, recommending to "just throw spinach in a buttered skillet for a bit and add mushrooms before the spinach starts to wilt. Then, let the spinach cook down and the mushrooms warm up. It's great on top of rice. Don't forget salt and pepper, too!" Carey adds that she likes to add sesame seeds and dried fruit after sautéing veggies.

Here's what I most frequently include in my rotation.

Green Beans, Mushrooms and Carrots

The idea for this recipe came from All Recipe's Green Bean and Mushroom Medley I make every Thanksgiving.[26] I adapted it to be a little healthier for everyday meals.

Serves: 4-6

Ingredients:
- 2 cups green beans, washed and cut
- 2 large carrots, cut into strips
- 2 cups mushrooms
- ½ onion, sliced
- ½ tsp. salt
- ½ tsp. garlic powder
- ¼ tsp. white pepper
- 2 Tbsp. olive oil

Directions:
1. Steam green beans and carrots until tender but firm.
2. In a medium pot, sauté onions and mushrooms until tender. Reduce heat, cover, and cook for 2–3 minutes.
3. Stir in green beans, carrots, salt, garlic powder and white pepper. Cover and cook on low for about 5 more minutes.

Mushrooms

For some reason, every time I sautéed mushrooms, I was disappointed with the results. My search for answers landed me on You Tube's "Make Perfect Sautéed Mushrooms" created by To Serve Men.[27] This was when I realized the error of my ways. First, I wasn't sautéing long enough for the mushrooms to reabsorb the oil. Second, adding a bit of soy sauce gave the mushrooms a burst of flavor. Whenever I have leftover mushrooms, I sauté them using this exact method.

Red Pepper and Broccoli Stir-Fry

The first time I tried Broccoli Red Pepper Stir Fry on Fruits and
Veggies More Matters website, I was hooked.[28] Powered by the
Produce for Better Health Foundation, the site has tons of ideas
for cooking with veggies.

Serves: 4

Ingredients:

- 1 Tbsp. olive oil
- 2 garlic cloves, minced
- 3 cups broccoli florets
- ¼ cup chicken or vegetable broth
- 1 large red bell pepper, cut into strips
- ½ medium onion, sliced
- 1 Tbsp. lemon juice
- ½ tsp. salt

Directions:
1. Add oil and garlic to a skillet over high heat. Once the garlic
starts to sizzle, add the broccoli and sauté until bright green.
2. Add broth, remove the skillet from heat and cover for 2 minutes.
Return to high heat and add the onions and pepper.
3. Sauté another 2–3 minutes. Remove from heat and mix in lemon
juice and salt.

Breaded and Raw

Young children prefer veggies that are crunchy. That's why
breading vegetables before roasting or serving them raw with a

tasty dip, can encourage kids to give it a try.

Zucchini Fries

My daughter has a thing for breaded and crispy food, which is why these zucchini fries are such a hit. I adapted this from Weekly Bite's Matchstick Zucchini Fries.[29]

Serves: 4

Ingredients:
- 3 zucchini, cut into small wedges or matchsticks
- 1 egg
- 3 Tbsp. milk
- ⅓ cup panko breadcrumbs
- ⅓ cup shredded Parmesan cheese
- a few grinds of fresh black pepper
- ¼ tsp. salt

Directions:
1. Preheat oven to 450°F. In a small bowl, whisk together the egg and milk.
2. In a separate bowl, mix together the remaining ingredients. Dunk the zucchini into the egg mixture, then coat with the breadcrumb mixture.
3. Place the breaded zucchini on a foil-lined pan sprayed with cooking spray. Bake for 25 minutes or until golden and tender.

Veggie Plate

Why not put out a veggie plate with ranch or hummus to dip as a side? I also like to do this when my kids complain of hunger before the meal. Any veggies will work: carrots, celery, sugar snap peas, broccoli, red bell pepper and cauliflower. Try it with store-bought or homemade ranch dressing on pg. 66.

Mix and Match

I assign sides for my rotation every week. I look at what we had last week and try to keep up variety. I assign a starchy side (bread is an option), at least one vegetable (cooked, salad or raw) and usually fruit. I consider the cooking method, so I'm not doing everything on the stove or oven (see chart below). Often, when I roast veggies, I do it ahead of time. If I'm not sure my kids will accept the main dish, I make sure they prefer at least one of the side dishes. If I can't figure out a good side, I put out bread.

Food Type	Tried and True with Cooking Method	Example Meals
Protein	*Stove:* fish cakes *Oven:* pork, lentils, fish, shrimp, chicken *Slow cooker:* chicken	Fish cakes, roasted potatoes, salad and apple slices
Starch	*Stove:* quinoa, mashed potatoes, couscous (pg. 113) *Oven:* roasted potatoes, brown rice *Rice cooker:* quinoa, rice	Pork tenderloin, quinoa, green-bean sauté and fruit salad
Veggie	*Stove:* green beans, carrots, mushrooms, broccoli, red pepper *Oven:* broccoli, cauliflower, asparagus, zucchini, veggie medley (seasonal), winter squash (pg 122) *Raw:* salads and raw veggie plate	Chicken, mashed potatoes, roasted broccoli and strawberries Salmon, roasted sweet potatoes with veggies (make ahead), salad and pears
Fruit	*Fall/winter varieties:* apples, pears, oranges, kiwi *Spring/summer:* apricots, oranges strawberries, grapes, melon, berries, peaches, plums, mango, papaya	Lentils, brown rice, mushrooms and seasonal fruit salad. Shrimp, quinoa, red pepper and broccoli stir fry and grapes

Cooking Jobs for Kids

Younger, beginner cooks (five years old and under) can:

- Learn about oven safety and cooking proteins (taking temperatures)
- Chop (and peel when needed) potatoes with assistance
- Assist with roasting and sautéing veggies

Older, more experienced cooks (six years old and over) can:

- Be responsible for cooking one part of the meal
- Prepare veggies and potatoes
- Make simple salads (challenge children to come up with their own!)

Goals

I'm always on the lookout for fish entrees. I'd also like to add a pork chop recipe to the mix and cook more with eggplant and sautéed greens.

Now let's move on to seasonal cooking!

10 SEASONAL MEALS

I live in San Diego where the seasons aren't very well defined. It does get cooler come fall, but we still have hot days well into October. During the winter, we have cool days where you might need a jacket instead of a sweater. Summer can be hot, but nights usually turn cool. This type of weather allows for more flexibility with food and what is available, but I still like to change dinners up as the seasons change.

Below are meals that are good for hot weather when you want to keep the oven off and send someone (in my case, it's my husband) to grill something. Having a handful of meal ideas for grilling protein sources and making simple side dishes is key.

Grilled Main Dishes

Below are the protein-focused, grilled items I include in our summer rotation.

Grilled Chicken Teriyaki

This has become our go-to marinade for grilling chicken. For quicker cooking, we use the same method described on page 57, cutting thick breasts in half and/or pounding until chicken is about

½-inch thick. I marinate the chicken earlier in the day.

Serves: 4

Ingredients:

- 1–1½ pound boneless, skinless chicken breasts
- 3 Tbsp. olive oil
- 3 Tbsp. soy sauce
- 4 garlic cloves, minced
- ½ lemon, juiced
- 2 Tbsp. brown sugar
- ½ tsp. salt

Directions:

1. Put chicken in a Ziploc bag and pound with a mallet until it's ½-thick. In a small bowl, mix the rest of the ingredients and pour over the chicken and seal the bag. Marinate the chicken in the fridge for at least an hour before grilling.
2. Preheat grill to high heat. Grill chicken, for 3-4 minutes per side, or until the chicken is cooked to an internal temperature of 165F.

Salmon or Other Oily Fish

Salmon or tuna steaks are perfect for grilling. We use our rub (pg. 88) to season fish or pair it with an avocado dip from All Recipes.[30]

Grilled Shrimp

We prefer using large shrimp to make it easier to maneuver on the grill. You could always use skewers and make kabobs. I get this marinating hours before grilling. It's simple, fast and tasty.

Serves: 4–6

Ingredients:
- 2 pounds raw jumbo shrimp, peeled and deveined
- ⅓ cup olive oil
- 2 Tbsp. lime juice
- 2 Tbsp. orange juice
- 2 cloves garlic, minced
- ½ tsp. onion powder
- ½ tsp. salt
- ¼ tsp. dried basil
- ¼ tsp. black pepper

Directions:
1. Put shrimp in a large Ziploc bag. In a small bowl, mix the rest of the ingredients and pour over the shrimp and seal the bag. Marinate the shrimp in the fridge for at least an hour before grilling.
2. Preheat the grill to high heat. Grill the shrimp for about 5 minutes, turning during cooking, or until they turn pink and are cooked through.

Turkey Burgers

This recipe is a nice base for grilling or cooking turkey burgers on the stove. I serve them with avocado, sliced red onion and lettuce. Adding Mexican spices, like cumin and chili powder, can work well, too.

Serves: 4–6

Ingredients:
- 1–1½ pounds ground lean meat
- ½ cup breadcrumbs

- 1 tsp. garlic powder
- ½ tsp. salt
- ¼ tsp. pepper
- 1 egg

Directions:
1. In a large bowl, combine the meat, egg, spices and break crumbs. Form into about six patties
2. Preheat grill to high. Grill turkey about 5 minutes on each side. If cooking on the stove, cook over medium-high heat for about 5 minutes per side.

Black Bean Sliders

To be honest, I typically bake this burger instead of grilling it. It's nice to have a veggie burger option.

Serves: 4-6

Ingredients:
- 1 14-oz can black beans, drained and rinsed
- 2 tsp. olive oil
- 3 tsp. taco seasoning mix (pg. 46)
- ½ tsp. salt
- 2 cloves garlic, minced
- 1 egg
- ⅓ cup breadcrumbs
- ¼ cup cilantro (optional)
- 1 medium sweet potato, cooked and mashed (no skin)
- ½ cup Mexican cheese blend (or cheddar)
- hamburger buns or tortillas

Directions:
1. Preheat over to 350°F or turn grill to high heat. Add beans, oil and spices to a food processor and pulse until chunky (not pureed).

2. In a medium bowl, mix the bean mixture, egg, breadcrumbs and mashed sweet potato until well combined.

3. Form this mixture into small patties for sliders (about 8–10) or larger ones (about 5-6) and place on a baking sheet prepared with cooking spray. If grilling, cover a large plate with tin foil, spray with cooking spray and top with patties. Brush each patty with some olive oil.

4. *Oven:* Cook for about 15 minutes. Flip the sliders and cook an additional 5–10 minutes or until lightly browned. *Grill:* place the foil topped with patties on the grill and cook about 5-8 minutes per side.

5. Serve with sliced tomatoes, avocado or guacamole, onions, buns or tortillas. If using tortillas, cut in the same shape as the patties and bake in the oven or fry in oil until crisp.

Grill Sides

Everyone needs a few go-to grill sides. I set out to master a bean, potato, whole-grain and pasta salad. I also wanted a grilled veggie side and fruit, of course.

Black Bean Salad

I love Black Bean and Corn Salad from All Recipes.[31] I decrease the oil and skip the corn. It's also a good option for lunches.

Roasted Veggie Couscous

This is adapted from Budget Bytes' Roasted Vegetable Couscous.[32] Of course, you could use another whole grain like rice or quinoa.

Serves: 6–8

Ingredients:
  • 2 Tbsp. olive oil

- ½ red onion, sliced
- 2 yellow squash, sliced
- 2 zucchini, sliced
- 1 red and 1 green bell pepper, cut into strips
- 4 garlic cloves
- salt and pepper, to taste
- ⅓ bunch parsley, chopped
- 2 cups uncooked couscous
- 3 cups chicken or vegetable broth

Directions:
1. Preheat oven to 400°F. Prepare the veggies and place them in a large bowl and add the oil. Mix until all the veggies are coated with oil.
2. Arrange the veggies on a large baking sheet (you might need two). Sprinkle with salt and pepper and cook for about 45 minutes.
3. Prepare the couscous according to package directions, replacing water with broth.
4. When the veggies are done, chop them up, mixing the garlic throughout.
5. Chop the parsley and mix it with the couscous and vegetables. Add more salt and pepper if desired. This can be served warm or cold.

Sweet Potato Salad

I'm not big into mayo-drenched potato salads, so I was on a mission to find a potato salad recipe that not only excluded mayo but included my favorite spud, sweet potatoes. This was inspired by Jessica Fishman Levinson's (at Nutritioulicious) Sweet Potato Salad.[33]

Serves: 4–6

Ingredients:
- 3 large sweet potatoes (2 pounds)
- 4 Tbsp. olive oil, divided
- 1 Tbsp. apple cider
- 1 garlic clove, minced
- 2 tsp. honey
- ½ tsp. Dijon mustard
- ¼ tsp. salt
- pepper, to taste
- ¼-½ cup cilantro, chopped

Directions:
1. Preheat oven to 400°F. Toss the sweet potato cubes with 1 Tbsp. olive oil and cook for about 30 minutes, stirring the cubes halfway through cooking.
2. Make the dressing by combining the remaining 3 Tbsp. olive oil, cider, garlic, honey, Dijon mustard, salt and pepper in a small jar, covering and shaking. If you can, do this hours or even a day before, so the flavors meld.
3. When potatoes are done, allow them to cool. In a medium bowl, gently toss the potatoes with the dressing and cilantro. Serve warm or at room temperature.

Grilled Veggie Skewers

Grilled vegetables are a must-have, and kabobs make it easy and fun.

Serves: 6–8

Ingredients:
- 8–10 wood or bamboo skewers

- 2 medium zucchini
- ½ pound mushrooms
- 1 red and 1 yellow bell pepper
- 2 yellow squash
- ½ red onion
- ⅓ cup olive oil
- 2 Tbsp. lemon juice
- 2–3 garlic cloves, minced
- 2 tsp. Italian seasoning mix (pg. 61)
- ½ tsp. salt
- ¼ tsp. pepper

Directions:

1. Soak the skewers in water for 30 minutes.
2. Wash and chop vegetables in uniform pieces. Cut stems off mushrooms, chop hard veggies in same round thickness, and cut onions into wedges.
3. Make marinade and mix with the veggies in a 9x13-inch glass dish. Cover and refrigerate for at least an hour.
4. Thread veggies onto skewers, alternating colors, and place back in the glass dish.
5. Grill vegetables on medium heat for about 10–15 minutes, turning and periodically and basting with leftover marinade.

Pasta Salad

A nice versatile pasta salad should be in everyone's rotation. Here's an easy base recipe:

Serves: 6-8

Ingredients:

- 4 cups uncooked tri-color pasta

- Italian salad dressing (pg. 65)
- 3–4 cups raw veggies of choice (zucchini, carrots, and celery work well)
- ½ red onion, diced
- ½ cup Parmesan cheese, finely grated

Directions:

1. Cook the pasta according to package directions and drain. Meanwhile, chop and prepare the vegetables.
2. In a large bowl, add the pasta, veggies, onion, salad dressing and Parmesan cheese. Add salt and pepper to taste.

Corn, Asparagus and Fruit Salad

Corn and asparagus are great additions to any rotation, but no recipe is needed. These are the easiest veggies to grill: just add some oil and salt.

With summer fruit being so tasty and juicy, I like to make different fruit salads. One of my favorite combinations is Tucson melon (looks like cantaloupe, but it has stripes), grapes or blueberries and strawberries. For a bit of fun, make kabobs using whatever fruit you have on hand.

Soups and Stews

As the weather turns cold, soups and stews hit the spot. I've tried many more than are listed here, but these are the ones that stuck. I prefer soups and stews with beans. My side strategy is to serve the following items with fresh baked bread.

Turkey Chili

Everyone likes something different in their chili. Carey says that "in the Midwest, we use pasta, typically elbows!" Feel free to adapt this, or any other chili recipe, any way you want.

Serves: 6–8

Ingredients:
- 1 Tbsp. olive oil
- ½ medium onion, chopped
- 1 pound ground turkey
- 2–3 garlic cloves, minced
- 2 15-oz cans kidney beans, rinsed and drained
- 1 can black beans, rinsed and drained
- 1 15-oz can of tomato sauce
- 2 cups chicken broth
- 2 Tbsp. chili powder
- ½ Tbsp. cumin
- 1 tsp. garlic powder
- 1 tsp. red pepper flakes
- ¼–½ tsp. salt (or to taste)

Directions:
1. In large pan, cook onion in oil for about 5 minutes. Add garlic for the last minute of cooking. Add the meat and stir until the meat is browned. Drain off the fat and transfer to a slow cooker.
2. Add the rest of the ingredients and cook on high for 3 hours or on low for 6 hours. Serve with toppings like cheese, sour cream and sliced avocado.

Lentil Soup

I love me some lentil soup. For a heartier meal, add chunks of cooked ham.

Serves: 6–8

Ingredients:

- 1 small or ½ medium onion, chopped
- 1 Tbsp. olive oil
- 2 large carrots, sliced
- 2 celery stalks, sliced
- 1 tsp. dried thyme
- 3 garlic cloves, minced
- 2 cups dried lentils
- 1 Tbsp. red wine vinegar
- 2 Tbsp. tomato paste
- 1 bay leaf
- 4 cups water
- 4 cups chicken or vegetable broth
- ½-1 tsp. salt
- Parmesan cheese (optional)

Directions:

1. In a large pot over medium to medium-high heat, cook onions in oil until just softened. Add carrots, celery and thyme and continue to cook until veggies softened, about 5 minutes. Add garlic for the last minute of cooking.

2. Add in lentils, vinegar, tomato paste, bay leaf, water and broth to the pot and mix until combined. Bring to a boil and then turn down the heat, letting it simmer for 20–30 minutes.

3. When lentils are cooked to desired consistency, add salt and remove the bay leaf. Top with shredded Parmesan cheese (if desired).

Ham and White Bean Soup

This recipe is adapted from Budget Bytes' Slow Cooker White

Bean Soup.[34] It is one of my favorite "meal" soups. I like to freeze
leftovers for lunches.

Serves: 6–8

Ingredients:
- 1 pound dried navy beans
- ½ pound carrots (about 4 large), sliced
- 4 celery stalks, sliced
- 1 yellow onion, diced
- 4 cloves garlic, minced
- 1 bay leaf
- 1 tsp. dried rosemary
- ½ tsp. dried thyme
- ½ tsp. smoked paprika
- fresh cracked pepper (10–15 cranks)
- 2 Tbsp. olive oil
- 7 cups liquid (half water, half chicken or vegetable broth)
- 2 cups cooked ham, chopped
- 1 tsp. salt (adjust as you taste)

Directions:
1. Rinse beans and set aside.
2. Chop veggies and add to a 6-quart slow cooker.
3. Add spices (except salt), oil and liquid to veggies, cover, and
cook on low for about 8 hours or until beans are soft but not
mushy.
4. Halfway through cooking, add the chopped ham. When soup is
done, add the salt and serve.

Veggie Soup

This is a good base recipe for cleaning out your fridge. In other words, adapt it anyway you want. Add your preferred spices, an acid (tomatoes, vinegar or lemon juice) and add-ins like noodles, pasta, beans and leftover meat, and you have a meal or side dish. You can always freeze it for later use.

Serves: 4-6

Ingredients:

- 1 Tbsp. olive oil
- ½ cup chopped onion
- 2 garlic cloves, minced
- ½ tsp. oregano
- ½ tsp. thyme
- ½ tsp. salt
- ¼ tsp. pepper
- 1 bay leaf
- 3–4 cups chopped veggies (celery, carrots, zucchini, peppers or other vegetables)
- 32 oz. broth
- 1 Tbsp. lemon juice
- 1 15-oz can white cannelloni beans, rinsed and drained

Directions:

1. Turn stove on medium-high heat and add oil and onions. Cook onion until tender, about 2–3 minutes.

2. Add garlic, spices and vegetables and continue to cook until veggies are tender.

3. Add broth and bay leaf and bring to a boil. Turn heat to low and cover for about 30 minutes or until veggies can be easily poked with a fork. Add beans and other add-ins for the last 10 minutes of cooking. If you are cooking tender veggies like greens or tomatoes, add halfway through cooking.

Slow Cooker Italian Chicken with White Beans

When I first started cooking, my mother-in-law got me a slow cooker for Christmas. It came with a *Better Homes and Gardens* cookbook. The recipe that I remembered most was the Italian Chicken with White Beans.[35] As I went through this meal-planning process, I immediately knew I wanted this recipe in my rotation. The first time I made this after a long hiatus, my daughter said, "this chicken is good." That was music to my ears.

Fall and Winter Sides

I like to incorporate different winter squashes when the weather turns cool. I know it's time when the grocery stores fill up with these amazing, colorful veggies. Many of the sides in Chapter 9 work in fall and winter too.

Spaghetti Squash: Thanks to Trader Joe's for this idea. Start by poking the squash with a fork about eight times, then cook it in the microwave for about 6 minutes. Turn the squash and cook it for another 3 minutes. When it's done, it should feel as soft as a ripe avocado. Cut it in half, remove the seeds, and scrape out the flesh with a fork to get spaghetti strings. You can add seasonings and butter for a side dish or use it as a substitute for spaghetti, topped with your favorite pasta sauce.

Mashed Butternut Squash: First, cut off the top, then cut the whole squash in half. Place the squash flesh side down in a 9x13-inch glass baking dish filled with an inch of water. Cover with foil and bake at 350°F for 50–60 minutes, depending on how big the squash is. When it's done, scoop out the seeds and then the flesh. Add some butter, brown sugar, cinnamon, or any other seasonings you like.

Roasted Winter Squash: For any winter squash, cut the squash in half and turn it flesh-side up. Top with butter and honey or brown sugar. Roast at 400°F for about an hour. Cut into big chunks and serve. Alternatively, you can cut the uncooked squash into cubes and roast with olive oil and any spices you enjoy.

Cooking Jobs for Kids

Younger, beginner cooks (five years old and under) can:
- Learn about grill safety and cooking proteins (taking temperatures)
- Rinse and soak beans
- Wash veggies

Older, more experienced cooks (six years old and over) can:
- Assist with grilling
- Assist with chopping veggies
- Make marinades
- Put together simple slow cooker meals

Goals

When summer rolls around, I'll be on the lookout for more grilled fish recipes. For winter, I would like to add a few more soups like a lighter version of cream of broccoli.

Now that the testing recipe part is complete, let's move on to the last section of the book.

PART 3: STOP AGONIZING OVER FAMILY DINNERS

"You will know you made the right decision; you feel the stress leaving your body, your mind and your life."

-Brigitte Nicole

11 SET UP AND TWEAK YOUR CORE MEAL ROTATION

This is the part of the process that will set you free. Free from stress about what to make. Free from frequent cooking mistakes (I can't promise none). Free from buying and stocking the wrong foods. Free from all the obstacles that happen when you don't plan ahead of time and figure out what you really want.

It's time to fit together all the pieces of your family-dinner puzzle. It really is simple: just take the meals you have mastered and decide how you want to rotate them.

Getting Started

There are different ways to go about implementing your core meal rotation. You can start from the beginning of the process, rotating your list of Tried and True meals while gradually adding to it.

Although all my meals weren't quite where I wanted them, I started with a rotation of 25 meals, making five per week. I included one for the weekend, even though I don't always make it. I usually cook Sunday, but sometimes we go to my mother-in-law's for dinner. I like having a meal planned just in case, and sometimes I make it anyway to freeze or use for Monday's lunch. On Saturday, we eat out unless we are entertaining. Below is my first stab at my core meal rotation. You can see how my rotations have evolved by visiting RaiseHealthyEaters.com/category/dinner-rotation.

Monday	Tues.	Wed	Thur.	Friday	Weekend
Chicken enchiladas	Spaghetti		Chicken tenders	Baked salmon	White bean and ham soup
Turkey tacos	Shrimp linguine	Kids' choice	Pork tenderloin	Pizza	Slow-cooker chicken and white beans
Quesadillas	Tuna casserole		Chicken teriyaki	Black-bean burgers	Baked shrimp
Fish tacos	Alfredo		Stir-fry	Lentil soup	Chili
Fajitas	Lasagna		Greek pitas	Salmon cakes	Curry

Things may look different for you, and that's not only okay, that's the way it should be. "We don't have a true rotation going yet, but keeping our favorite recipes in one spot has been a life saver," says Jen. "Plus, it allows us to write notes about the changes we've made, or shortcuts to use, and side dishes to make with the main dish." Carey is nervous about cutting down her meals, but she's going to give it a try, cooking new recipes on the weekend. "We have chosen 25, categorizing them by your suggested nights and found agreement in much of your nights and categories… we'll keep working on it."

Key Elements of Your Core Meal Rotation

As detailed in Chapter 3, one key formula of my rotation is organizing by theme: Monday is Mexican, Tuesday is Italian, Wednesday is kids' choice, Thursday is square meal or ethnic and Friday is just something easy. Depending on the pace of the weekend, meals can be a bit more involved or easy. Weekends can also be a good time to bring kids in the kitchen.

When making my rotation, I always take into account nutritional variety. For example, I try to get at least one seafood dinner a week, beans and legumes a couple times, and a decent variety of fruits and vegetables. Each week I assign sides I want to cook, including salads. This way, when I'm shopping, I make sure I have all the ingredients on hand and can even get a head start preparing them on the weekend. This helps decrease waste, especially when it comes to fresh produce. I also make the best meal choices with my kids' activities in mind. Late practices may call for a slow-cooker meal. If my husband or I work late, that's another consideration. Each week, I double-check the meals in my rotation to make sure they match any changes to our schedule. When there's a conflict, I simply swap out meals.

There are other ideas that might work for you that I chose not to do. One is cooking a big chicken (or other type of meat) on Monday and using the leftovers throughout the week. You may want fewer or more meals in your rotation. Some people prefer cooking large batches of meals one day and freezing them to use throughout the month. A new trend is to swap meals with other parents. Basically, depending on how many people are in the group, you make that number of the same meal and come together to exchange meals. You go home and freeze your meals for future dinners.

Regardless of the different ways you go about rotating your dinners, the key is just to get started and see how it goes. Your rotation will never be perfect and contain everything you want, but once you start, you will see how it needs to be changed.

Make Your Rotation Visible

I print out each new version of my rotation, putting it on the fridge for everyone to see. If there are any complaints, I tell my kids I will consider it as I revise it the next time. I also like to take notes on the back of the printed page about what worked, what didn't work, and any changes I can make for next time.

Meghan laminated a template to make her weekly meals visible, writing on it with a dry-erase pen. Carey uses a dry-erase board in her kitchen that includes a week's worth of meals. "I put my ideas on it on Sunday, and I have found it saves me continually from veering off the plan," she says. "Lots of times, we reinvent and switch a day or accommodate a last-minute change, but this really helps guide my husband and me."

The first week I followed my rotation, I made every meal and felt a calm come over my week. Cari felt this way, too. "This week, I actually had a plan for every day, so my mental space felt more relaxed," she said.

The more familiar I became with each meal, the more prepared I felt as the dinner witching hour approached. I was able to gradually add in jobs for my kids, even if the task was done way before mealtime. One strategy that worked for Miranda was telling her kids that if they helped with dinner, they could choose one item that would go on the table. "They might add a bowl of nuts or a certain fruit they're in the mood for," she says. "This not only gives them something on the table that they like, but it also creates a more positive mood around the meal."

Tweaking Your Rotation

Modifying your rotation just kind of comes with the territory. As I'm writing this, it's summer, so I just updated my rotation to reflect summer meals, removing soups and stews, and I'm working on some staple grill sides. I'm still testing new recipes, jazzing up current meals and deciding which meals to let go, even if it's just to take a break for a while.

Every time my five-week rotation is done, I consider what changes need to be made by checking any notes on the back of my printed rotation. Overtime, these changes have become pretty minor and are a lot less work than traditional meal planning.

Dinner Goals

It's important for me to consistently check in with my personal cooking goals. I think about the type of meals that are needed to balance things out. Sometimes I practice a new cooking skill by checking out videos on You Tube, or I look for ways to change or enhance a meal I've gotten pretty decent at making.

I also look for meals to capitalize on my kids' new tastes. For example, if one of them adds a new food to their repertoire, that can spur my interest in developing a new meal. For example, my six-year-old's acceptance of turkey tacos led to getting turkey burgers on the menu. My daughter's love of croutons in salad led to new salads *with* croutons.

If you fear getting bored of your rotation, remember it is not static. It should evolve and change right along with your family's needs and preferences.

Evolving Shortcuts

Keep an eye out for short cuts that evolve from your rotation. Here are the time-savers that have really helped me:

- Create homemade spice mixes
- Make sides and main dishes ahead and freeze them
- Prep for dinners during breakfast, lunchtime or at night
- Develop specific shopping lists based on where food is located in grocery stores
- Create an end-of-the-week "clean fridge" day

- Have a prep day, either Sunday or Monday, to replenish stashes of salsa, spice mixes, marinara sauce or anything planned for the week
- Buy a cooking gadget that helps make preparation better and faster

I don't want to give you the impression that mealtime is perfect in my home. I wish! But it is improving a little more every day. When I look back to where I started, the change is significant.

The best thing about reaching this point is you can *stop agonizing* over what to cook for dinner. Instead, you can focus on mastering the meals you and your family love.

12 CREATE YOUR OWN COOKBOOK

I n my last traditional job as a dietitian, I often encountered couples with grown children who stopped cooking for themselves. They talked about how they used to cook when their kids were around, but transitioned to eating out when it was just the two of them. Sadly, they realized they should have kept cooking as I educated them about how and what to eat after having a heart attack.

Now that I'm in the trenches of family cooking, I can understand why they stopped. Often, making meals for a family isn't much fun. Compound this meal dread by 18 plus years and it's no surprise that burnout results. The technology age makes this worse because everyone seems to be doing a better job at it than you. Perfectly crafted meals are plastered all over the internet. Family cooks in the public eye go on about how their kids eat exotic meals simply by being asked to take a bite. All the apps, sites and online meal planners should help but somehow the struggle remains. It's all too easy to get a complex and feel like you're just not measuring up.

But, of course, this is all an illusion. The perfect family meal and dinnertime doesn't exist. Yes, some parents have superb cooking (and photography) skills but that is not needed to make family meals a success. There is room for all types of cooks and meals. What's most important, but often overlooked, is keeping the cook happy.

This book is all about throwing yourself into your meals and figuring out what you want. It's about streamlining the process because you don't want to spend more time than is necessary in the kitchen (unless you want to, of course). It's about making reasonable goals, so you can improve a little bit every day. It's about exposing your children to a good enough variety of food while helping them grow into respectful table guests and decent cooks. I want every single one of you to keep cooking when your kids are grown up because it has become a bright spot instead of a pain that finally goes away.

Each Person's Journey is Different, but the Principles are the Same

I started this process of simplifying well over a year ago. Packaging it nice and neatly in a book can make it seem like it should be a quick and painless task, but that was not the reality for me, and it probably won't be for you, either. No doubt, if I had this book to guide me, it would have significantly cut the time it took and mistakes made. That's why I wrote it for you. So, depending on your starting point, you may get through this process pretty quickly or be working on it for several months. There's no right or wrong, just your journey.

Although where you end up may be different, this book is based on these common principles:

Simplify Your Meals: You should have a streamlined list of meals that work for your family, a workable kitchen and goals for new meals that make it easy to find winner recipes. If you start to feel overwhelmed, it may be that simple has turned chaotic. Just go back to Chapters 1–4 to get back on track. Keep trying different formulas, like theme nights, to simplify meals.

Strategize Your Cooking: Don't let recipes find you, find the right ones instead. In other words, don't forget your goals when adding new meals. If you are stumbling in one area, take the time to find out what you need by educating yourself. But most of all, be kind and patient with yourself.

Stop Agonizing Over Family Dinners: Maybe you discover implementing a rotation has saved your life, or you'd rather plan weekly meals from your Tried and True list. It doesn't matter as long as what you are doing is working. By working, I mean that family dinners are no longer a struggle. Instead, they feel organized, doable and generally satisfying.

The Best Cookbook in the World is Your Own

After years of buying other people's cookbooks, I thought it was time to make my own. Plus, I got tired of looking at my sad, three-ring binder of printed recipes. I had been eyeing make-your-own cookbook companies and wanted a nice storage and easy reference for my Tried and True recipes.

I chose the Cookbook People because they have a variety of cooking binders to choose from. I also love being able to enter, change and print out recipes using their software. I don't have to wait for an order to come in, which is ideal for a rotation cookbook that's always changing. There are other make-your-own cookbooks on the market, so feel free to look around.

If you prefer, there are plenty of online storage sites for recipes, too. Meghan has been using Plan to Eat, an online meal-planner, for about two years. After reading this book, she created tags for Tried and True, In Between and Want to Make meals. "Using these tags, I will try to include at least one Want to Make in every week, possibly two if our weekend is quiet," she says.

And using a combo of online and print resources is fine, too, as long as it doesn't get overly complicated. I personally prefer having something physical to look at while I'm cooking, and I don't want to rely on having an iPad charged because, knowing me, it won't be charged at that crucial time. Plus, I'm a very messy cook, and techy gadgets are not supposed to get food on them!

When you're ready to actually make your own cookbook, you are in a good place. That means you have enough meals to be excited about and rotate for good variety. With your own cookbook in hand, you can take back all the energy that used to go into agonizing over what to cook for dinner. I know this purposeful way of cooking has greatly improved my family's quality of life, and I hope it has done the same for you.

"There is definitely less stress in our house about what's for dinner, and we are eating healthier than we used to, not using all the boxed meals like we used to fall back on," says Jen after simplifying and strategizing her meals.

Although you've reached the end of this book, your role as the family cook is far from over (even after the kids are gone, right?). My wish for you is that dinnertime becomes your family's happy place. And, even more importantly, that you never, ever have to agonize over what to cook for dinner again!

ABOUT THE AUTHOR

Maryann Jacobsen is a registered dietitian, independent author and speaker. She is founding editor of Raise Healthy Eaters, a popular blog about family nutrition. Her writing has appeared in Huffington Post, New York Times Motherlode, Los Angeles Times, Mind Body Green and She Knows. As a family nutrition expert, she has been quoted in various publications including *Parents, Scholastic Parent & Child* and *American Profile* and has been featured on *Good Morning America.*

Other titles from Maryann include:

From Picky to Powerful: The Mindset, Strategies and Know-How You Need to Empower Your Picky Eater: In this book, you'll learn the scientific reasons *why* most children become picky in the first place—and the importance of individual differences—so you can understand your child's eating behaviors. Jacobsen outlines specific and effective strategies for feeding your child based on the latest research. The result? Peaceful meals, more connection, and better eating over the long haul.

Fearless Feeding: How to Raise a Healthy Eater From High Chair to High School: Considered the bible of feeding kids, you'll get the *What, How* and *Why* of feeding at each stage of development — infancy, toddlerhood, school age, adolescence and adulthood. You'll learn *what* to expect in terms of growth, child development (the *why* of eating) and *how* to meet nutritional needs.

Sign up for Maryann's email list to be notified of her new books and free offers: RaiseHealthyEaters.com/list.

APPENDIX A

Worksheet 1: Discover What Works and What Doesn't

The first step to simplifying your meals is developing laser focus.
You do this by identifying what's working, what isn't and why.

What you will need:

- Cookbooks, magazines and any other cooking resources
- Access to all your stored and printed recipes
- Three-ring binder
- Folder

1. Start with your cookbooks, magazines and online recipe
resources. Which do you really use? Giveaway or unsubscribe to
what doesn't excite you.

2. Go through all your recipes discarding those you know just
won't work. If you are torn, say you like the meal but you don't
make it often, keep it in a separate folder. Your goal is to identify
and list out what I call your Tried and True recipes. These are your
favorite go-to meals. When you are done, store these in your three-
ring binder.

Tried and True:
1._____
2._____
3._____
4._____
5._____
6._____
7._____
8._____
9._____

10._____

11._____

12._____

13._____

14._____

15._____

16._____

17._____

18._____

19._____

20._____

3. Look at your Tried and True list and examine the why behind what works. What is it about these meals that makes them stick?

Preparation/time:_____

_____

_____

_____

_____

Popularity:_____

_____

_____

_____

_____

Ingredients:_____

_____

_____

_____

_____

Other
reasons?_____

_____

_____

_____

_____

When you are done, you should have:

- Three-ring binder with your Tried and True recipes (or stored somewhere else)
- Folder with recipes that need some work
- Your most treasured cooking resources stored close by

APPENDIX B

Worksheet 2: Streamline Your Kitchen

In this second step to simplifying your family dinners, you'll want to dive into your cabinets, fridge and freezer asking one very important question: *What is in here and do I actually use it?*

What you'll need:
- Completed Worksheet 1 with your list of Tried and True meals

Make a list of what you want to stock: Take your Tried and True list of meals and add items your family eats for breakfast, lunch, snacks and dessert. These are the foods you want to keep stocked in your kitchen.

Breakfast:

_____

_____

_____

_____

Lunch:

_____

_____

_____

_____

_____

Snacks and Dessert:

_____

_____

_____

_____

✓ **Go through your cabinets:** Sort through your pantry throwing out any past date stuff. If it isn't on your list of stocked items, give it away or store it off site. The goal is to only have on hand items you use with regularity. Same goes for cookware.

✓ **Go through your fridge and freezer:** Examine each item in your fridge and throw out what is old, paying close attention to all those condiments on the side. Do the same with your freezer. Toss or giveaway anything you just know you aren't going to use.

✓ **Make handy lists:** Make organized lists for food storage to do inventory before shopping trips.

✓ **Store food properly:** To keep food waste down, download and print my comprehensive food storage list at RaiseHealthyEaters.com/what-to-cook-for-dinner-templates. This is an ideal time to reorganize your kitchen the way you want it.

When you are done, you should have a well-organized kitchen with easy access to the food you love to cook.

APPENDIX C

Worksheet 3: Create Your Meal Vision

In this final step to simplifying your family dinners, you'll close the gap between where you are now, and where you want to be. You do this by creating your meal vision.

List your cooking and meal preferences. Do you like quick prep or something more involved? Lots of ingredients or simple? What type of food and ingredients do you enjoy cooking with the most?

_____

_____

_____

_____

What is important to you in terms of nutrition and health? What is missing in terms of variety? Need more veggie dishes? Lacking fish entrees?

_____

_____

_____

Note each family member's food preferences and how you can build meals based on what your child already likes.

_____

_____

_____

Choose a formula to organize dinners whether it be theme nights, a side strategy or serving meals in a particular order.

_____

_____

_____

Develop a list of meals you want to add to your Tried and True list. In Between meals are the recipes you kept in a folder in Step 1. The items on your Want to Make list are the meals and sides that fill in what's missing.

In Between:
1._____
2._____
3._____
4._____
5._____
6._____
7._____
8._____
9._____
10. _____
11._____
12._____
13._____

Want to Make
1._____
2._____
3._____
4._____
5._____
6._____
7._____
8._____
9._____
10. _____
11._____
12._____
13._____

NOTES

1. Heffernan, Virginia. "What if You Just Hate Making Dinner." *The New York Times Magazine*. The New York Times Magazine, 8 October 2014. Web. 27 November 2015.

2. Marcotte, Amanda. "Let's Stop Idealizing the Home-Cooked Family Dinner." *Slate*. Slate, 3 September 2014. Web. 27 November 2015.

3. Tanofsky-Kraff M, Hyanos HL, Kotler LA, Yanovski JA. Laboratory-based studies of eating among children and adolescents. *Curr Nutr Food Sci.* 2007; 3 (1): 55-75.

4. Kondo, Marie. *The Life-Changing Magic of Tidying Up*. Berkeley, California: Ten Speed Press; 2014.

5. "Kay Toomey, PhD." *SOS Approach to Feeding*. SOS Approach to Feeding, 2015. Web. 27 November 2015.

6. Satter, Ellyn. "Division of Responsibility in Feeding." *Ellyn Satter Institute*. Ellyn Satter Institute, 2015. Web. 27 November 2015.

7. "Restaurant Style Salsa." *Pioneer Woman*. http://thepioneerwoman.com/cooking/restaurant-style-salsa/

8. "Have it Your Way Tacos." *Meal Makeover Moms*. http://mealmakeovermoms.com/recipes/mexican-tonight/have-it-your-way-tacos/

9. "Hidden Valley The Original Ranch Dressing Copycat Recipe." *Top Secret Recipes*. http://www.topsecretrecipes.com/Hidden-Valley-The-Original-Ranch-Dressing-Copycat-Recipe.html

10. "Simple Shrimp Scampi with Linguine." *Weekly Bite*.

http://weeklybite.com/recipes/simple-shrimp-scampi-with-liguine/

11. "Slow Cooker Veggie Lasagna." *Raise Healthy Eaters.* http://www.raisehealthyeaters.com/2010/04/family-dinners-slow-cooker-veggie-lasagna/

12. "Thin Crust Pizza." *Pizza Making.* http://pizzamaking.com/thincrust.php

13. "Real Chinese All Purpose Stir Fry." *Recipe Tin Eats.* http://www.recipetineats.com/real-chinese-purpose-stir-fry-sauce/

14. "Crockpot Chicken Teriyaki." *Wannabite.* http://wannabite.com/crockpot-chicken-teriyaki/

15. "5 Steps to Making Fabulous Fried Rice." *The Asian Grandmothers Cookbook.* http://theasiangrandmotherscookbook.com/2011/10/07/fried-rice-recipe/

16. "Red Thai Curry Sauce." *Pinch of Yum.* http://pinchofyum.com/red-thai-curry-sauce

17. "Baked Salmon II." *All Recipes.* http://allrecipes.com/recipe/34746/baked-salmon-ii/

18. "Pork Tenderloin with Seasoned Rub." *Food Network* (Ellie Kreiger). http://www.foodnetwork.com/recipes/ellie-krieger/pork-tenderloin-with-seasoned-rub-recipe.html

19. "Brown Rice and Lentil Casserole." *Food.com.* http://www.food.com/recipe/brown-rice-and-lentil-casserole-74629

20. "Olive Oil Mashed Potatoes with Garlic." *Cook for Your Life.* http://cookforyourlife.org/recipes/olive-oil-mashed-potatoes-with-garlic/

21. "Honey Roasted Sweet Potatoes." *Food Network* (Ellie Kreiger). http://www.foodnetwork.com/recipes/ellie-krieger/honey-roasted-sweet-potatoes-recipe.html

22. "Baked Brown Rice." *Food Network* (Alton Brown). http://www.foodnetwork.com/recipes/alton-brown/baked-brown-rice-recipe.html

23. "Heating Olive Oil." *The Olive Oil Source.* n.d. Web. 27 November 2015. https://www.oliveoilsource.com/page/heating-olive-oil

24. "The Best Broccoli of Your Life." *Amateur Gourmet.* http://www.amateurgourmet.com/2008/11/the_best_brocco.html

25. "Roasted Garlic Cauliflower." *All Recipes.* http://allrecipes.com/recipe/54675/roasted-garlic-cauliflower/

26. "Green Bean and Mushroom Medley." *All Recipes.* http://allrecipes.com/recipe/25285/green-bean-and-mushroom-medley/

27. "Make Perfect Sautéed Mushrooms" *You Tube* (To Serve Men). https://www.youtube.com/watch?v=BEWu3d3v_tU

28. "Broccoli Red Pepper Stir Fry." *Fruits and Veggies More Matters.* http://www.fruitsandveggiesmorematters.org/main-recipes?com=2&recid=40

29. "Matchstick Zucchini Fries." *Weekly Bite.* http://weeklybite.com/recipes/matchstick-zucchini-fries/

30. "Grilled Salmon with Avocado Dip." *All Recipes.* http://allrecipes.com/recipe/47569/grilled-salmon-with-avocado-dip/

31. "Black Bean and Corn Salad." *All Recipes.* http://allrecipes.com/recipe/13933/black-bean-and-corn-salad-ii/

32. "Roasted Vegetable Couscous." *Budget Bytes.* http://www.budgetbytes.com/2011/08/roasted-vegetable-couscous/

33. "Sweet Potato Salad." *Nutritioulicious.* http://www.nutritioulicious.com/2013/05/sweet-potato-salad-a-new-twist-on-a-summertime-favorite-recipe/

34. "Slow Cooker White Bean Soup." *Budget Bytes.* http://www.budgetbytes.com/2013/09/slow-cooker-white-bean-soup/

35. "Slow Cooker Chicken with White Beans." *Raise Healthy Eaters.* http://www.raisehealthyeaters.com/2015/01/30-meals-slow-cooker-chicken-with-white-beans/

Made in the USA
Middletown, DE
20 July 2017